CUBICLE
WARFARE

Self-Defense Tactics for
Today's Hypercompetitive Workplace

BLAINE L. PARDOE

PRIMA PUBLISHING

PRIMA PUBLISHING and colophon are registered trademarks of Prima Communications, Inc.

Disclaimer   This book covers controversial office politics. Some of the tactics discussed in this book may be considered illegal, unethical, or immoral. Prima does not condone or endorse these tactics. Any reader who decides to use any such tactics does so at his or her own risk.

Library of Congress Cataloging-in-Publication Data

Pardoe, Blaine Lee.
    Cubicle warfare: self-defense tactics for today's hypercompetitive workplace / Blaine Pardoe.
        p.   cm.
    Includes index.
    ISBN 0-7615-1066-4
    1. Office politics.   2. Success in business.   I. Title.
HF5386.5.P37   1997
650.1'3—dc21   97-20427
                                                                            CIP

97 98 99 00 01 HH 10 9 8 7 6 5 4 3 2 1
Printed in the United States of America

How to Order

Single copies may be ordered from Prima Publishing, P.O. Box 1260BK, Rocklin, CA 95677; telephone (916) 632-4400. Quantity discounts are also available. On your letterhead, include information concerning the intended use of the books and the number of books you wish to purchase.

Visit us online at www.primapublishing.com

To my wife, Cyndi;
my kids, Victoria and Alex;
and my parents, Rose and Dave.
They were all very supportive during the
writing of this book.

To G. Gordon Liddy, whose radio show
I listened to at lunch when I managed to edit a page
or two of this. Nothing like listening to someone who's
been there and done that.

And finally to Central Michigan University,
home of the mighty Chippewas.

With love to
Lisa, who shouldn't
have to fight so
hard! me neither...
Anne '98

CONTENTS

CONTENTS

ACKNOWLEDGMENTS

I want to acknowledge my agent, Ethan Ellenburg, who had the guts to help me get this book marketable. I also want to thank Paula Lee at Prima for giving me that burst of encouragement in the middle of this book. Thanks also to Debra Venzke at Prima.

Special thanks to Dan Plunkett and Cullen Tilman, who helped me many a Sunday to make sure that I didn't miss any tricks. Also thanks to Ed and Barb Wilson for not thinking that their son-in-law was some sort of weird mutant strapped to his PC.

I also acknowledge my neighbor, Greg Johnson, for his appropriate twisted sense of humor.

INTRODUCTION

Politics is too serious a matter to be left to the politicians.

Charles de Gaulle

This book is not for the weak of heart. In fact, it's every business ethics teacher's worst nightmare. It is the embodiment of the corporate world's greatest fear. The reason? This book details the seamy underside of corporate America, documenting the internal office politics that takes place every hour of every day in every company. Understanding these previously unwritten rules of the game will help you survive a career's worth of assaults, and it may well propel you on to your own greatness and power.

There are other reasons as well. Office politics causes the loss of millions of dollars of productivity every year, though no formal study will ever reveal how much because so many managers blatantly lie about the fact that politics exists in the first place. Unknown and unnamed thousands lose their jobs every year because of backstabbing politics waged by corporate managers or partners vying for power. Countless projects worth billions in revenue are sabotaged, scuttled, buried, or lost in committee every year because of office politics.

So why not simply abolish this cutthroat behavior? Because you can't. It is ingrained in the business community more deeply than the concept of expense accounts. Also—much like Congress's control over its own salaries—the people with the most control over politics are the most political animals out there. It is a cancer that permeates the body of the business world, and the treatment to remove it would kill the patient.

Thus office backstabbing and butt kissing have become a form of necessary evil. We've all seen it at some point in our careers. What's important is to learn more about it—to master ways to see the bullet coming at you and somehow dodge it.

That's what this book does.

Writing this tome is taboo in the eyes of many executives. This discussion is like picking at a scab that no one wants to admit even exists. For what it's worth, *reading* this book should be considered worse than the writing of it.

What you will find in the following pages are the strategies and tactics that many individuals use to work their way up the proverbial corporate food chain. Most of these are, unfortunately, not fiction, but the real-life stratagems that employees and managers use every day to carve out a living in corporate America—if not all over the planet.

HOW TO USE THIS BOOK

War is hell, or so General Sherman said. He was right. What most people don't realize is that the offices of the world are a place of constant warfare—a war of the political nature. Calling it *office politics* is polite and takes some of the bitter edge off, but in the end it is a war. *Cubicle Warfare* is designed to be a guide. It outlines the warring factions, defines the strategies and tactics that are deployed, and gives you, the reader, the hope of becoming something more than a mere casualty.

This book will give you the "tools of the trade" when it comes to the world of politics in the workplace. It lays out the background necessary to build your own political strategy, then overviews the tactics needed to survive war in your company or firm. The book is designed to be read from beginning to end—but if you're in a rush to get a jump on your internal office competition, feel free to skip ahead to the tactics section so that you can begin your education as soon as possible.

Your tutelage begins with an overview of the battlefield—the office—where politics takes place. It is useful to understand how your corporate organizational structure and hierarchy contributes to or interferes with the political games around you. This section also covers how to analyze what marks true power in your company—and how to leverage it to your advantage.

Covered next is how to recognize your potential enemies—in other words, the chudlike co-workers and peers who are fighting for a place in your company. (Bear in mind that *chud* refers to fish parts that are chopped up and fed to sharks. You do not want to be chudlike.) With all this background, you will finally be ready to sculpt your overall strategy for political accession.

This book details the myriad political tactics that are prevalent and possible. As sad as it may be, many of these are tried-and-true tactics—things that actually work. Obviously not all of them work in every situation, but—depending on your company's structure and political environment—you are bound to find some useful weapons here.

Finally, once you have studied the strategies and tactics of the game, you are ready to study your foes. Detailed in the final section of the book is a listing of the various types of political players you are likely to encounter in a typical firm or corporation. Understanding your enemies will help you survive your encounters with them, or defeat them as you seek to establish a toehold in an organization.

DISCLAIMER

My agent, my publisher, my wife, and a handful of close friends all insist that I cover myself here. Their fears are well founded. Put this book into the hands of the weak and corrupt, and havoc could result. Unimaginable hours of lost productivity in thousands of corporations. Careers crashing down in flames. Lawsuits hither and yon.

We wouldn't want that to happen, would we?

So the contents of this book are solely for the purposes of instruction, study, and entertainment. The author, publisher, printer, and the guy working in the mail room all assume that everyone on the planet is an adult. If anyone actually does any of the sleazy and borderline illegal (well, outright illegal) things described in the book—well, it's on their head. You're just reading to protect yourself, right?

Also, all the examples in this book are true—though the names have been changed to protect the guilty. I swear that I can defend every instance and can name names and point fingers as proof that the examples are exactly what happens in the real world—not the sterile world of college textbooks and ethics classes.

GETTING STARTED

First, forget everything you ever learned regarding the modern business and corporate environment. What you know, even if you've been exposed to politics and backstabbing, is the proverbial tip of the iceberg. This book is a guide, peeling back the layers of what *really* happens in offices around our planet every hour of every day. You need to know this stuff either to survive or to succeed—whichever path you choose.

Break out the aspirin and scotch and prepare for the ride of your life. What follows is many nights' worth of cold chills and deep-seated paranoia, the results of having witnessed countless acts of political terrorism over the years.

Be prepared, be ready. It's only the fight of your life.

WHAT IS OFFICE POLITICS?

Internal office politics is an ingrained part of every organization in some form or another. What is this faceless nemesis? Frankly, *internal politics,* for purposes of this book, refers to those actions by individuals or entities in any organization that are aimed at personal or group advancement rather than meeting the objectives of the company or firm as a whole.

A number of components of this definition are worthy of explanation. Politics is not simply a personal matter, though more often than not it manifests as such. In corporate environments, entire departments, divisions, practice areas, and so on often compete against each other for the limited resources available.

Another element of the definition is that internal politics is based on advancement despite company goals and objectives (and sometimes even those of the clients or customers). Politics, even negative smear campaigning, is aimed primarily at advancing one person's career or pushing a group to prominence in some fashion. Company or firm goals do not matter in the eyes of the corporate politician unless they can be used against specific intended targets.

WHY LEARN THIS GAME?

Depending on the organization and the individuals there, millions of dollars may be wasted on internal politics. Over and above the money, countless hours are lost to internal politics every day. And finally, a tangible amount of energy is lost as well—energy that is diverted from productivity or profitability of the company to personal or departmental gain.

To succeed as a manager or supervisor, it is critical to harness this energy. Understanding the ways of those who play the game of company politics allows a manager to use this wasted energy for the betterment of the firm. Bottom line, knowing the rules of the game gives you at least a chance to win.

And there is the survival factor that comes into play. Simply put, politics touches everyone who works in offices. Like listening to Howard Stern, everybody does it and nobody admits it. You can't dodge politics, nor can you avoid its touch if you go to work every day. It is better to learn about how office politics works than be a victim.

And don't kid yourself, there are victims. Lots of them. Some manage to get away with just a few moral scratches, while others lose their careers, homes, and livelihoods and end up on the streets. For every successful executive, there is a body count of those who got walked on to pave the way to that big corner office.

Even if you are a person who takes no active part in politics, knowing how the game is played means that you stand a good chance of surviving the depredations of those who undertake a lifestyle of cubicle warfare. This is a book that helps you avoid becoming a victim. Instead, you can turn yourself into a survivor of the constant (and often pointless) warfare waged in organizations around the world.

A WORD ON "POLITICAL CORRECTNESS"

And that word is *puke!* Political Correctness (PC) is a concept aimed at making everyone feel happy about who they are—leveling the proverbial playing field. Politics breeds like mushrooms in horseshit in that sort of environment, thriving and spreading while people claim they're only trying to be fair to each other.

As you may have guessed, political correctness is not something you are going to see a lot of in this book. I tend to call things as I see them. If, for example, we're going to talk about homosexuality in the workplace, I'm going to call it that—not *alternative lifestyles.* If that's too hard for you to deal with, too bad, you've already paid for the book. Pass it on to one of your blunt and non-PC friends to enjoy—then watch your back. If you are politically correct and the subject of corporate politics intrigues you enough to risk your pristine and misplaced mental energies, then check out the section titled Corrupting and Contorting Company Resources, Procedures, and Political Correctness in Chapter 6.

Bottom line: This is a book about surviving the deadliest game of all—office politics. If you're too hung up on using pretty words and making the world safe for seals, dolphins, or whatever, this is probably not going to be a pleasant experience for you—but an eye-opening one to be sure.

WHAT THE HELL QUALIFIES ME TO WRITE THIS?

> Politics is not a bad profession. If you succeed there are many rewards, if you disgrace yourself you can always write a book.
>
> **Ronald Reagan**

Simply put, I have been there and done that. I once thought I'd seen it all when it comes to office politics, but that's not possible. The truth is that I am not that big of a political player, but I've paid close attention over the years—much to the apprehension (and regret) of my former managers.

My background? I've worked either directly for or outsourced to all three of the Big Three auto manufacturers. I've worked with and around the infamous Beltway Bandits common to the Washington, D.C., area, who live like ticks off the blood of the taxpayers. Finally, at the time of this writing I work at one of the Big Six accounting firms. Altogether I've seen politics in corporations, firms, and in the dark alleys of every city I've had to travel to.

I've seen the damage that politics can wreak. In some cases I've taken part—even successfully in some instances. I've also been a victim of managers (and I use that word loosely) and the bizarre political games that they played. I've watched people's careers burn to a crisp and scatter to the four winds. There've been massive layoffs, individual firings, and "partings of the way" around me, all in the name of conducting business, all tainted heavily or motivated by petty office politics. I've given people ulcers simply by putting my hands on their political games, and yes, a few people have lost their jobs because of me.

So why am I qualified? I've been in the trenches like you. I've taken out a few fat-bellied corporate politicos in my years as well. I've been shot at myself—and hit a few times, too, but I've managed to survive and do pretty well. More important, I want to make sure that no one needlessly or mindlessly stumbles into the mistakes I made in my various careers.

Read on. I'm sure that there are few real surprises in the pages that follow. I think any laughing you do will be uneasy, given that all this is based on the real world.

Politics: (noun) From Greek, *poly,* meaning
many, and *ticks,* meaning *bloodsuckers.*

Anon

THE BATTLEFIELD

Politics, in the form of office politics and cutthroat behavior, exists everywhere. Some environments foster this kind of behavior more than others, much as damp places breed mold and mildew. Before you can begin to lay out your own political strategy or determine what tactics you wish to opt for, you must understand the area where you will be fighting. In other words, know the terrain of the cubicle warfare battlefield.

This is not just a study of how your company reacts to politics, it's an overview of the key elements that politics feeds on. Understanding these elements is critical even if you do not wish to wage an offensive political campaign. You want to survive, don't you?

This chapter includes a test to determine your company's level and degree of politics. It will serve as a measuring instrument to determine what kind of cubicle warfare environment you work in.

ow Is Power Measured? Knowing what defines power is important—and measuring it is something that is almost of equal consequence. Every company on the planet has its own way of determining or gauging how much power someone has. Sometimes the index is tangible (such as a unique benefit or perk), sometimes it is perceived (such as having a slightly more desirable office than a peer).

Here is a sample of the ways many companies measure power:

- Number of personnel reporting to a manager or department—the classic headcount power index.
- Prime location (building or floor).
- Company-paid country club memberships.
- Company-sponsored trips and promotional meetings.
- Window or corner office.

POWER

pow·er ('paù(-ə)r) *n.* **1.** The ability or capacity to act or perform effectively. **2.** Often powers. A specific capacity, faculty, or aptitude. **3.** Strength or force capable of being exerted: might. **4.** The ability or capacity to exercise control: authority. —*The American Heritage Dictionary of the English Language*

pow·er ('paù(-ə)r) *n.* **1.** The results of successful cutthroat politics. **2.** The ability to alter the lives of others regardless of their own desires or designs. **3.** Exertion of control with a lack of morality or guilt. **4.** The reason to come to work every day. See Authority. —*Cubicle Warfare*

- Amount of budget controlled by manager.
- High-profile projects assigned to a manager.
- Most profitable customers assigned to a manager.
- Number of ceiling tiles in office or office space.
- Executive or exclusive parking spots.
- Better class of office furniture.
- Better executive perks (human resource-based benefits).
- Company car.
- Extended vacations.
- Most powerful computer hardware or system (if system is technologically oriented).
- Bonuses for performance or profitability.
- A higher degree of acceptance by upper management for failures. (Where others would die, you merely get scolded or less.)

Power is what politics is about. For some, it is the means of getting things done. It is a form of security. For others, power is a way to maintain control not just of their careers, but of the careers and lives of others.

That is not to say that power is the root of evil or that politics itself is evil. Without power, things in any company would never get done. Important documents would not be signed, people would not get paid, and so on. However, in the hands of someone adept at manipulating politics, power becomes something more. Like a master tactician or strategist, a political maven will use politics to ensure personal success. Your job as a manager is to go beyond this and ensure not just your personal success and career, but that of your company, division, department, team—anything whose success will enhance your own.

THE TERRAIN

In a physical sense, terrain consists of the features of the earth that define the landscape. In the arena of office politics, *terrain* consists of aspects of the company or firm that you work in. Political terrain works like the hills and trees of a battlefield— where there are obstructions, you move around them. They define where you work, and in many respects, govern the types of tactics that you can employ.

This section will explore a number of different factors that define your political battlefield in a typical corporation or firm. Here are the key terrain features that you are likely to encounter:

- The type of company you work for
- The formal and informal organizational structure
- The seats and paths of authority
- The leadership style of your management
- How communication is managed
- The definition of power and where it resides

Company Type

There are three primary forms of business, each with its own particular strengths and weaknesses in terms of politics and political behavior. While there are no hard and fast rules as to how political an organization is based on its type, Table 1.1 sets out some useful guidelines and notes some general tendencies.

TABLE 1.1. Political Potential.

Type	Characteristics	Potential for Politics
Proprietorship	Sole owner Usually small company	Low. To play politics in this organization you have to sleep with the owner or the owner's spouse (or both).
Partnership	Owned by two or more partners Can be large (2,000+ partners) Liability is spread among the partner-owners	Moderate, usually depending on size. Larger Limited Liability Partnerships (LLPs) like the Big Six can offer a ripe environment for politics. Smaller partnerships can also have a high degree of potential depending on how they are managed. In the end, the number and names of owners are known and all have a direct management of the business meaning that, in the end, they control the overall politics of their firm.
Corporation	Owned by stockholders Largest companies on the planet are corporations The breeding ground for management trends and politics	High. Corporations have a lot of plausible deniability when it comes to politics. The deeper the infrastructure and the older the company, the more chance of facing corporate politics.

Organizational Structure

More often than not, this is usually defined by a management tool known as the organizational chart, or *org chart*. In most companies the org chart that is in place bears only slight resemblance to how the company is truly shaped and organized.

Instead, the chart itself is a tool for showing other managers how the organization *should* look—though the real lines of power, authority, and communications often do not follow the boxes and arrows shown on the chart.

In terms of politics, there are two areas where organizational structure comes into play. One is the overall number of levels in the organizational chart at its deepest possible point. The more levels an organization has, the more apt you are to be exposed to politics. The other is where you are in this written documentation in terms of those levels.

In Figure 1.1, it is easy to see that the Midwest doesn't have as many levels as the other areas. Therefore, the opportunity for politics is dramatically less than in the other areas. While there are other factors that mitigate or contribute to internal politics, fewer levels mean less of a breeding environment for internal politics.

Age of the Business

The age of a business often helps contribute to the political environment that you may be caught up in. Young companies tend to concentrate so hard on the external environment—coping with pressure for rapid growth, survival against their competition, and so on—that would-be political players don't have the time or inclination for internal politics. Also, there is not a great deal of history that people can leverage in power plays.

Companies that emerged in the early Baby-Boomer era and have several decades under their belts have become somewhat stagnant—despite what they may publish in their annual reports and press releases. Such companies, for the most part, are perfect environments for politics. Companies that are several

	President North American Operations		
	Vice President East Coast	Vice President West Coast	
North Area Manager	Midwest Area Manager	South Area Manager	Coastal Area Manager
State Managers (One for Each State)	State Managers (One for Each State)	State Managers (One for Each State)	State Managers (One for Each State)
Office Managers (One–Four for Each State)	Office Managers (One–Four for Each State)	Office Managers (One–Four for Each State)	Office Managers (One–Four for Each State)
Office Administrator (One for Each Office)	Office Administrator (One for Each Office)	Office Administrator (One for Each Office)	Office Administrator (One for Each Office)
Manager (Two for Each Office)	Supervisor (Three for Each Office)	Manager (Two for Each Office)	Manager (Two for Each Office)
Supervisor (Three for Each Manager)	Associate (Ten for Each Supervisor)	Supervisor (Three for Each Manager)	Supervisor (Three for Each Manager)
Associate (Ten for Each Supervisor)		Associate (Ten for Each Supervisor)	Associate (Ten for Each Supervisor)

FIGURE 1.1. Sample Org Chart.

hat Is This Authority Stuff and Where Do I Get Some? Authority in most companies comes in two flavors. The first is *legitimate* authority. This is often known as paper authority. It is usually based on position in a company or firm and is related to powers formally vested in an individual because of that position. An example of this is the manager who can sign off on purchase requisitions of $10,000 or less. This is a formal authority defined by the position.

The other flavor of authority is *real* authority. It is defined as *the unacknowledged means of accomplishing tasks within a company.* This is not spelled out anywhere in an employee handbook, but is the informal and often covert

decades old have enough history behind them to allow their employees, especially middle-level managers, to make use of this history for their own political plans and agendas.

Older companies (more than 50 years old), especially larger ones, offer the biggest opportunities for internal politics. They have been around so long that their histories have become traditions. With a depth of history that is difficult to duplicate, such firms offer a potential politician an environment that cannot be surpassed. Older managers often support a "Good Old Boy" philosophy in promoting and advancing underlings, which forces competition and backstabbing on a broad scale.

Size of the Company or Firm

Bottom line: the bigger the company, the more dangerous its political potential is. A small company with a staff of ten, while it may have some politics, cannot compare with a large multiway that most companies actually function and survive. For example, the manager mentioned earlier has a secretary who has the power to make sure that your purchase requisition actually ends up on the desk of said manager for signature. The secretary can make that happen—or lose the requisition, bury it in a pile of paperwork, or even shred it and claim that you never dropped it off in the first place. While the manager has legitimate authority, the power (oftentimes unspoken) of the real authority figures is what keeps the cogs of the great corporate machine grinding along—for you or over you.

national corporation with thousands of employees in terms of the risks of being exposed to or being used in politics.

Geographic Scope of Your Company

One of the factors that contributes to the use of politics is the use of multiple buildings, multiple plants, or multiple locations. Having geographic separation, even of a few meters, is often enough to break down nominal communications between groups.

Visibility of Upper Management

The accessibility and visibility of upper management—a feature of corporate culture as much as individual preference—helps define how close management is to the day-to-day operations of

as It Always Like This?   Did Cubicle Warfare always rage in offices or is this simply a sign of our times? The truth is somewhere in the middle.

In the post–World War II era, people who worked at a company often bought into the concept of "a job here for life"—that is to say, as long as they were loyal and did their jobs, they'd always have employment. There was a symbiotic approach to living and working in a company. Everyone was happy—on the surface.

Politics existed but it was more subdued. Since long-term *careers* were on the line (not like *jobs* today), politics was akin to boxing—with all the formal rules. Blood was drawn, but few died in the ring. This was going to change, just like the "evolution" of boxing into Ultimate Fighting.

Two things changed this. First was the thrust of union power in the '50s through the '70s, when the employees developed the notion that if a company made profits, those profits belonged to the line workers rather than the company. Look at the union contracts and the raise scales during this period. Gouging was commonplace. Companies began to see the employees not as part of the team, but as part of the problem. Staff became an expense rather than a requirement.

the business. It generally defines how closely upper management interacts with the clients or customers as well.

In terms of its impact on politics, generally the more removed management is from the workers at the front lines of the operation, the more likely they are to play political power games with their employees' careers, projects, and lives.

During the same period, companies that never thought of laying people off before had to do so because of the recession, oil embargo, and assorted other problems. Suddenly it dawned on some corporations that they could make do with fewer people and survive.

Then began the concept of outsourcing . . . the moral decline of the corporate world. Start letting go of entire departments and replace them with other people. Once this trend kicked in, employees saw that after 25 years of hard work, they could be booted onto the street with three weeks' severance. Attitudes changed. People started leaving companies and changing jobs—people who never would have considered that two or three decades earlier.

And with this came the rise of cubicle warfare in the office. *Why not stab the boss in the back? After all, the bastard might lay me off in the next round of hits anyway. And hey, if all goes bad, I'll leave and get a job somewhere else.*

In other words, our society created the environment for office politics and cubicle warfare—now it is a matter of survival to learn the ways of the cubicle warrior and beat this nefarious system.

The Impact of Outsourced Labor

One of the most amusing trends in current management is the practice of outsourcing labor. In this, you lay off your own staff and outsource the labor to a vendor who provides the bodies to do the task. Oftentimes, the vendor will actually hire the same

here Does Politics Come From? The root of politics is competition. Yes, competition. Throughout our entire lives, we are schooled and instructed on how to compete. From spelling bees to football games, competition is pumped into every fiber of our bodies. Even those who claim they are not competitive have been exposed to enough political machinations throughout their lives that they cannot totally resist the urge to take part.

Once we enter the day-to-day work world, we find the need to advance. But there are fewer and fewer spaces available as you move up the corporate food chain, so you

people you laid off (albeit at a lower wage) to perform their old jobs.

How does this relate to internal politics? Simply put, outsourced labor, no matter what spin a company may try to put on it, is generally a source of bodies. In the contemporary corporation, these personnel represent an interesting challenge. They often hold key positions and have access to power, while at the same time they have absolutely no long-term vested interest in the success or well-being of the company. This means that they are a rogue element in the politics that takes place. Their risks in taking part in political affairs are often low, buffered by the fact that they do not work for the company in the first place. Added to that, such individuals often possess power (real or perceived) that other employees covet.

PERSONNEL TURNOVER AND POLITICS

Turnover in a company is a self-fulfilling prophecy in terms of politics. A high rate of turnover allows a political player to

need to distinguish yourself from your peers if you want to attract the kind of notice that will move you into one of those widely coveted spots. And how is this done? Politics. It is a way to stand out in a crowd. Using politics is a seductive means of competing against your peers. If anything, using politics makes you feel part of your company environment—part of the team.

And resources are limited in any company. Only so many dollars are available for projects, programs, and headcount. Thus jockeying for these limited resources only adds to the air of competition—a breeding environment for politics.

bring in new staff, corrupt and seduce other managers' staff, and add new players to the game of politics (often referred to as "fresh meat" by true political players). Thus a high turnover rate adds to the potential for you to be exposed to politics in your day-to-day activities.

On the other hand, the more politics there is in a company, generally the more disgruntled employees there are (the losers and the mindless slugs caught up in the political scenarios that are being crafted and executed around them). Harboring the ill-born belief that they will one day find a job devoid of internal politics, the disgruntled employees leave. Thus the cycle of employee turnover feeds more politics, leading to more turnover. . . .

COMMUNICATIONS

Communications has several different aspects. The first is formal communications—things such as memo distributions,

anagement Programs in the '90s and Beyond A number of programs are marketed to management in companies. These have a direct impact on areas like employee morale and careers. However, management often

Program or Concept:	Concept as Sold by Marketing Departments of Consulting Firms:
Business Process Reengineering (BPR)	Review business processes from the ground up and essentially change how the organizations operate. The noble goal is to increase productivity, decrease costs, and increase client satisfaction.
Change Management	This usually consists of a series of training events (deprogramming sessions) aimed at teaching your staff to deal with change more rapidly and effectively.
Total Quality Management (TQM)	Empowering the employees to take control of their work processes to improve quality. Oftentimes this involves setting up "self-directed work teams," which are empowered groups of employees who attempt to change how work is done to make it more realistic, sensible, high-quality, or quick.

(deliberately or otherwise) fails to explain what these programs mean to the individual. While all the programs offer the potential for increased politics, it is important to understand the downside of such programs.

Reality:*

- Reorganizations (often on a large scale).
- Layoffs (in most cases).
- Increases in outsourcing.
- Changes in processes that don't work in your company.
- Changes in processes that do work but suddenly stop functioning.
- Total chaos if your management is not strong enough to control the effort.

- Layoffs. Usually Change Management is used as a veil for "Some of you aren't going be around any more, but we want you to *feel good* about it, okay?"
- Reorganizations. After all, you don't teach people to change unless you plan on messing things up in the first place, right?

- Bitterness toward management when the employees in the majority of these programs realize that they don't have any real authority to make changes.
- Work slowdown. With everyone working on changing their processes, nobody has much time for the real job.
- Chaos. Self-Directed Work Teams often turn into Self-Deworked Wreck Teams.

continued

continued

Program or Concept:	Concept as Sold by Marketing Departments of Consulting Firms:
Co-Partnering / Co-Sourcing / or Anything starting with prefix "Co"	Rather than take on a management task all on your own, partner with another company or firm; essentially outsource some of your operations to improve your chances for success.
Downsizing	Reducing unnecessary headcount from an organization.

*While not mentioned in the Reality column, all these programs make a lot of money for the consultants hired to do the work, and most implementations of them damage employee morale. Also, such programs invite

newsletters, e-mail regarding new clients, press releases, and so on. A common misconception regarding formal messages is that they are devoid of politics. The truth of the matter is that they are more calculated, more scripted, more precise than other messages—usually due to the politics behind them. Also, the release of formal communications, who gets what information and when, is often a very controlled and manipulated process. Example: "Didn't you get that memo about the new re-organization effort? Oh, I'm sorry. . . . "

Informal communications systems are much more intricate and vital to the success of a political effort in a company or

Reality:

- A concept that is about as sound as "My ship is sinking. If I strap another sinking ship to mine, we'll both float."
- Mistrust and blame. Both "co-partners" will seek to blame each other for the failure of the project, rather than the consultant who proposed it.
- Where there are failures, there are layoffs.

- One word—layoffs.
- Usually you can spot a poorly executed "downsizing" effort by the fact that perfectly worthless middle-level managers somehow keep their jobs while individuals who work hard and produce are mysteriously let go.

individuals to assume new authority and power—further adding to the complexity of politics that an individual might face.

firm. Informal communications, most commonly referred to as "the grapevine," is not traditionally controlled by management. It is a grassroots effort on the part of individuals to disseminate information through less than formal means. Sometimes this is in the form of gossip or rumors, other times it can be useful confirmations or nonconfirmations from individuals who do not hold formal positions of power.

The grapevine is, by and large, more efficient and faster than formal communications; it deserves the attention of every would-be politician. The reasons are simple. If you do not master the informal communications in a company, they can work against you even if they are not being manipulated by your opponents. Most important, control of formal communications is defined structurally in a company or firm; that is, it is well known who can issue press statements in a given company or who can send out a memo regarding employee vacations. Informal communications are often controlled by individuals who do not have true authority in a company, only access to power. An example of this would be the executive assistant to a vice president that drops hints to fellow administrative assistants as to what projects are about to be approved. While on a paper org chart an executive assistant rates fairly low in the pecking order of a company, he or she can spread communications regarding projects, people, and careers faster than a wind-whipped wildfire.

While every company has formal communications, informal communications systems are in place almost any time there are more than four people working in an office. Oftentimes, where two or three formal communications channels are in place, dozens of informal communications networks exist. Grapevine systems are virtually impossible to control. They cannot be killed by order or edict from management—if anything, this only gives them additional credibility. The true political aficionado will take advantage of the systems; the novice will simply become either a victim or a participant in the informal communications process. *Note: Chapter 5, The Art of War— Cubicle Style, covers the control and use of the grapevine in politics.*

BUZZWORD PROGRAMS AND FADS

Nothing new has been created in the arena of business management in the last few decades. The last thing created that was considered new was the way to market management concepts by assigning them acronyms or buzzwords. This was done by authors more intelligent and less scrupulous than this one, who did it to make money. Some of these programs, including Business Process Reengineering (BPR), Total Quality Management (TQM), Empowerment, Change Management, and several others, exist to do nothing more than reduce overall employee productivity and increase the potential for politics in a company.

If such programs exist in your company, the potential for your exposure to internal politics is high. People worry about their careers, jobs, organizational structures, management reporting, and so on. Many have built political empires and such programs place those empires at risk.

COMPANY MYTHOLOGY AND LEGENDS

Learning the unofficial history of politics in your company or firm is important because the actions in the past often reflect the culture of your company. This history does not have to be all that accurate; history usually gets distorted by the victors and the survivors. But even twisted and distorted history can tell a great deal about the way your company deals with internal politics.

For example, if you have heard a story about Manager Bob who was allegedly demoted after an incident regarding a secretary and a sexual harassment allegation, this tells you that your company protects its upper management, even against charges that might normally result in dismissal. Or it can indicate that Bob must have had some information in his possession that allowed him to survive such an incident. Checking how the company handled similar complaints, usually through the grapevine, can help you flesh out a closer truth. Oftentimes, the informal communications network will provide a number of theories or opportunities to allow you to arrive at some strong conclusions.

POLITICAL EXPOSURE TESTING INSTRUMENT

> Those who are too smart to engage in politics are
> punished by being governed by those who are dumber.
>
> **Plato**

Politics is often compared to radiation exposure. You can survive a little bit easily, and a moderate dose may even serve as therapy. However, a massive dose is poisonous, even fatal. One of the questions asked by most people who are attempting to cope with internal company politics is, "What is my risk of exposure?"

While no true scientific testing instrument can be used to measure such exposure and determine exactly how internal politicking will affect your day-to-day life, it is possible to determine with some degree of accuracy how much exposure you face. That is to say, what is the frequency, opportunity, and potential for you to witness or take part in internal backstabbing and cutthroat politics in your company? (*Regardless of your willingness or desire to do so. . . .*)

What follows is a simple test aimed at determining this potential—your risk of political sandbagging. On the lighter side, it also defines the potential for you to take part in internal corporate politics.

This test presents two sets of factors. One is the infrastructure of the company—the physical factors that promote or inhibit political action around you. The other factor is related to the corporate culture of where you work. In other words, does your office promote an atmosphere where politics can thrive?

Instructions

Answer each of the questions that follow. At the end of the questions is an analysis session that allows you to determine the type of environment, culturally and physically, that you work in and how it may be a breeding ground for cutthroat behavior.

Questions

1. Age of business:
   a. 1–4 years
   b. 5–20 years
   c. 21–40 years
   d. 41–60 years
   e. 61+ years

2. Type of business:
   a. Sole proprietorship
   b. Partnership (2–12 partners)
   c. Partnership (13+ partners)
   d. Corporation

3. Number of levels of organization (at its greatest depth):

a. 3 or less

b. 4–5

c. 6–7

d. 8–9

e. 10+

4. Size of company or firm (personnel):

a. 5 or less

b. 6–100

c. 101–2,000

d. 2,001–6,000

e. 6,001+

5. Geographic placement or scope of work done (that is, where the work you do is performed for your clients or customers):

a. Local

b. Statewide

c. Regional (2–10 states)

d. National

e. Multinational

6. Number of business units, divisions, large departments, and so on in your company or firm:

a. 2

b. 3–4

c. 5–6

d. 7–8

e. 9+

7. Number of buildings where your company or firm has personnel:

   a. 1

   b. 2–5

   c. 6–10

   d. 11–25

   e. 26+

8. Times per year you physically see any of the top ten executives of your company or firm:

   a. 4+

   b. 2–3

   c. 1

   d. None

9. What percentage of your current department or division is outsourced consultants or labor?

   a. None

   b. 1%–10%

   c. 11%–20%

   d. 21%–30%

   e. 31% or more

10. What is the approximate staff turnover in your company or firm?

   a. 1%–5%

   b. 6%–20%

   c. 21%–25%

   d. 25%–30%

   e. 31% or more

11. Number of times office politics come up in conversation in a typical week:
   a. None
   b. 1–2
   c. 3–4
   d. 5–6
   e. 7+

12. Number of promotions or firings you've heard attributed to politics:
   a. None
   b. 1–2
   c. 3–5
   d. 6–10
   e. 11+

13. Number of rumors you hear in a given week:
   a. None
   b. 1
   c. 2–3
   d. 4–10
   e. 11+

14. Number of managers you know who have been promoted or not dismissed for failed projects or company initiatives:
   a. None
   b. 1–2
   c. 3–5
   d. 6–10
   e. 10+

15. Does your company have a TQM (Total Quality Management) or BPR (Business Process Reengineering) initiative currently under way?

    a. Yes

    b. No

16. Time since your department, division, or company last reorganized:

    a. 25 months or more

    b. 12–24 months

    c. 7–12 months

    d. 1–6 months

    e. Never

Scoring

Total up your score based on your selections for questions one through eight, then separately for questions nine through sixteen. Scoring for your answers should be as follows:

    a = 1 point

    b = 2 points

    c = 3 points

    d = 4 points

    e = 5 points

Make sure to total both sets of answers. That is, you need the total for the first eight questions and a separate total for the last eight questions.

hat About Profit? Doesn't That Matter? One question that commonly comes up during a review of this instrument centers on profits for a company—usually in the guise of "Do profits factor into corporate politics?"

The answer is, bluntly, no. Politics occurs in a company regardless of whether it is making money or on the verge of bankruptcy. Why? The grim reality is that average workers in the modern company usually have little idea of

The Political Exposure Grid

> Being in politics is like being a football coach. You
> have to be smart enough to understand the game
> and dumb enough to think that it's important.
>
> **Eugene McCarthy**

Take your total score for questions one through eight and plot it on the Political Exposure Grid (Figure 1.2) on the horizontal (X) axis by drawing a line straight up from the point that matches your score. Then plot your total on the last eight questions on the vertical (Y) axis of the grid by drawing a line across the grid at the level of your score.

The dotted lines divide the Political Exposure Grid into four quadrants, labeled the Safe Zone, the Playground, the Old Boys' Home, and the Minefield in Figure 1.3. Your score lines will intersect in one quadrant or another, and the spot where they cross is a pretty good indicator of your current exposure to cubicle warfare. Of course, there are always exceptions to the rule; you may be in a high-politics quadrant but have a manager who

their overall impact or worth. They don't know what they contribute to the proverbial (and often elusive) bottom line. Those who do know usually end up either as partners (in LLPs or other partnerships) or out on their own, starting their own companies. *(Why share the profits with the lofty overheads of a corporation when I can keep everything for myself?)*

runs such effective interference for you that you and your staff are protected or filtered out of politics. On the whole, however, the findings are fairly accurate. Note your location, then read on to see the dangers and thrills that may be lurking around the corner or hiding near your drinking fountain. . . .

Safe Zone   Of all of the quadrants you can end up in, this is the most desirable if you don't want to take part in politics—or the worst if you want to be a player in the great game. Here the physical aspects of the company or firm that you work for do not support a great deal of political play; at the same time there is little evidence that your company's culture promotes or rewards those who take part in backstabbing or other nefarious activities common in internal politics. Many new companies or those going through rapid growth fall into this category.

Playground   In this quadrant and environment, the physical aspects of the company don't support political play, but the culture does. Morons (or worse) can get promoted based on

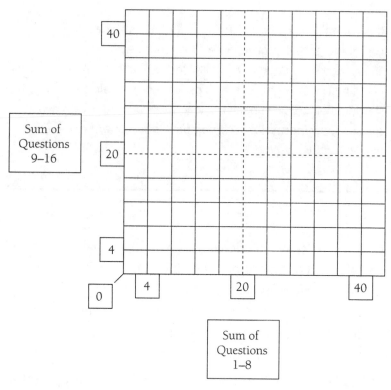

FIGURE 1.2.   Political Exposure Grid.

how they play the game. There is a rich history of political play and it is well known that if you want to get ahead, you have to play politics.

Usually in the Playground there are a handful of political leaders in the company or firm who are sponsoring this attitude and belief system in their staffs. Like feudal lords squabbling over ownership of a swamp, these managers wage a war of backstabbing over the number of ceiling tiles their departments have. It's petty, it's insignificant, but it's a way of life.

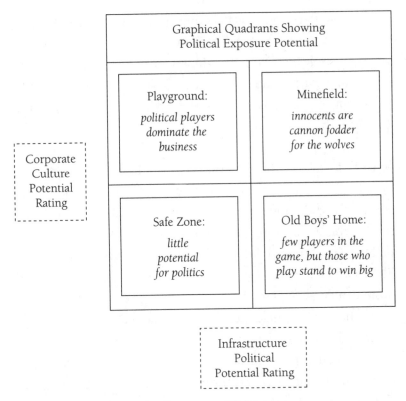

FIGURE 1.3.   Political Exposure by Quadrant.

Old Boys' Home   In this quadrant, everything about the culture of the organization indicates that it does not support politics, but the sheer size and scope of the company allows for political infighting. Almost always these are larger companies with strong infrastructure safeguards such as a review and promotion system that actually works to not reward those who simply play politics. Mindset of the Old Boys' Home—John Grisham's *The Firm:* a great place to work as long as you didn't try and play in the political game. If you do play, plan on playing hard and seeing a body count along the way.

There still are some players, however, taking each other on to fight over resources in these larger companies and firms. What most of the "Old Boys" don't realize is that it isn't necessary to take part in the politics they wage; they feel the need to play politics simply because of the size and complexity of the company they are in.

Minefield   Here the environmental and cultural factors not only endorse and encourage politics, they require it for sheer survival. For the innocent, mindless slugs who make up most of the typical workforce, this type of company is a fragment of hell that has surfaced and thrived on Earth. Darth Vader would like to work in this kind of place. A simple trip to the bathroom can be a dangerous political journey.

It is no small coincidence that state and federal governments fall into this arena. They are massive in terms of physical offices and infrastructure, while at the same time, the culture supports kissing up to the boss and those higher in the proverbial food chain. While on paper it appears that the organization is fair and just, in reality it is those who take part in politics who rise to the top rungs of the ladder. J. Edgar Hoover, for example, began as a simple entry-level administrator. In the course of a handful of years, he took over the FBI, dramatically expanding its scope and power to the point that it was a dominant force in American politics and lifestyle for decades.

Is there hope if you are stranded in such a place? Of course. The following chapters outline how you can manipulate the forces of politics around you to keep yourself safe—or even take advantage of the opportunities that offer themselves to the cubicle warrior.

> It is difficult to say who does you the most mischief: enemies
> with the worst intentions or friends with the best.
>
> **E. R. Bulwer-Lytton**

ASSESSING
THE OPPOSITION

I n any given office or corporate environment, some individuals take part in politics. Spotting these individuals is
important for two primary reasons. One, they are potential enemies who may oppose you. And two, they are candidates for
you to manipulate to your own means. Either way, spotting the
enemy and taking advantage of his or her strengths and weaknesses is something that has to be done early in your career lest
you become a victim rather than a victor.

If you don't want to take part in politics, this information is
still useful. It provides a pattern of where politics ebbs and
flows through your company or firm. Understanding how the
political players strike—and where—provides you with a mental map of your own political minefield.

Whom do you suspect to be a political player? It is not always easy to determine who might have political ambitions or tendencies at a first glance. Blatant political offenders stand out. The more artful cubicle warriors, however, are like serial killers; they look and act like everyone else, blending in with the crowd. This makes them all the more dangerous and worthy of study.

THE ICONS OF POWER

As discussed earlier, power is measured in many different ways in different workplaces. The index may be who has the bigger office, the better office position (say, the corner with the best windows), the closest reserved parking space, the bigger or newer company car, or any of a number of other small and not-so-small distinctions. These items are referred to as the *icons of power,* since they represent the tangible and visible means for figuring out who is in power and who is not. Like the trappings of a king or queen (the crown, signet, and so on), these icons are how you spot those in power. And the link between those who are in power and their role in politics is usually firm and hard.

While it's an ugly truth, few people rise into power cleanly. Once you understand how power is measured in your company, you can look at who holds that symbol currently as an indicator of who is in power. Chances are pretty good that these individuals understand politics and have manipulated their way into their current positions.

This is not always the case. Sometimes people do move into positions of power on pure merit. It is strength of character, leadership, and so on that has allowed them to rise into those positions. The odds of this happening in a typical organization, however, are somewhat less than those of being kidnapped by aliens. In reality, even those with true leadership qualities have had to use politics to fend off others, defend themselves, and even simply maintain their current positions of power.

There are those who stumble into greatness or power as well, but the odds are even less that this can happen. A typical example of this is the new sales representative who suddenly walks into a customer's office at the right time and lands millions in sales—and gets thrust rapidly into a position of power as a result. Usually these overnight wonders peak rapidly and then enter a period of decline as their detractors slowly and methodically erode their power and instant prestige. They get picked apart by the political vultures until their status is all but gone.

THE FASTEST FLIERS

Another useful barometer for locating potential political opposition is to determine who is on the rise the fastest . . . and why.

Promotions are, in many cases, driven by politics. If the people who have been promoted are not political aficionados themselves, they are usually those who either pose a threat or possess information that makes them useful to those in power. That being the case, it is important to look not just at who gets promoted, but who *benefits* from such promotions.

NATURAL POWER CENTERS

The natural power centers in a company are those projects or clients that are of the most importance to the company or firm. These are referred to as natural power centers because the employees who control them hold some measure of formal power in the organization. As the old line goes, those who control the purse strings control the company. *Such is the case,*

romotions—What They Really Mean The concept of promotion is one that predates business and has its origins in the military . . . one of history's first organizations with multiple levels of authority and power. On paper, a promotion is a reward for performance, an elevation to a higher level of responsibility.

In the office, promotions have become tainted over the decades. Instead of rewards or honors for those who perform well, promotions have evolved into a practice for establishing bases of power and authority. Below is a list of what promotions have become in the contemporary office:

- *A means of dealing with performance problems.* Rather than promote the most competent, managers often move the least competent up into positions where they have less and less power or authority. This is especially true if you can get a problem employee to take or receive a promotion into someone else's department.
- *A method of keeping employees subservient.* Guilt plays a big role in promotions. Promote people and they feel indebted to you, thankful, thus starting them down the path of being pawns in your own political game.
- *A way to appease the peasants.* Not everyone can be promoted . . . or at least that's the line that the HR Department orders most managers to recite. By promoting

except where politics are involved—a force that acts to redistribute power along other lines.

Who controls the bigger-profile projects or has the largest customers is important. They got there either by pure luck or, more likely, as a reward. Such rewards are often politically mo-

someone, you are sending a message to the staff that they should stay on board. The light at the end of the tunnel is hope—not an approaching train.

■ *Cripple thine enemy.* A quick way to cripple a political opponent is to take away key staff. An offer of a promotion in your piece of the organization often provides that key. It is not uncommon for a mediocre manager in a company to have an outstanding staff. When this is the case, it can almost always be attributed to the way that manager has managed to lure in the right staff with offers of promotion and advancement . . . in the process, hamstringing competitors for power in the company.

■ *Keeping problem children close.* In your career some of those who work for you are likely to expose or find information that could be turned against you. By using promotion as a tool, you elevate them closer to your level—where you can keep an eye on them. As a corollary to this, if you can promote them high enough—that is, to a level where they are clearly incompetent—none of your political enemies will think of taking them from you. To an outside opponent, it will look as though these potentially dangerous individuals do you more harm where they are than they could elsewhere.

tivated favors. Or the people in control created the illusion that they were working hard, generated enough political power to maintain that illusion, and as such were handed the projects or clients. Identify those individuals up front and you will know who has cut their teeth on the political teething ring.

THE BODY COUNT

Find the body count and trace it to its source. For every ruined career, every firing, there is someone who has benefited from it. Political actions in a company often result in body counts. This does not mean necessarily a string of people who have left the company more or less involuntarily . . . although sometimes that is the case. More subtle politicians don't leave such a blatant or obvious trail. Oftentimes the body count is a string of people whose careers have been trashed or who have found themselves removed from key projects, large client accounts, or leadership positions.

Locating the bodies is part of it. As in a murder investigation, you must ask yourself the key questions: Who stood to benefit from this demise? Did this injure someone or some project? Did this reduce the contenders for a promotion? Politics is rarely waged for sheer pleasure, and for every action (someone quitting or being fired) there is an opposite and powerful reaction (someone getting promoted or removing the competition). When you have tracked down who benefited from the political act, you have managed to determine someone who might one day consider you either a target or a potential ally.

THE GRAPEVINE

Management of communications, especially the informal communications of your organization (the rumor mill or grapevine), is a critical skill for any manager. Where formal communications fail or falter, the grapevine can often operate smoothly—and usually faster.

Oftentimes an office coup d'état is announced formally in the form of a reorganization letter or announcements of new promotions and advancements. The grapevine should always be used as a source to determine who, if anyone, really benefited from the results of such actions.

The grapevine also provides vast insights to plans that are already set in motion but have not yet reached fruition. The informal communications network often does what formal memos and e-mail cannot: it names names and points fingers. Tapping into the grapevine is useful to find out not only who is in power now, but who is aspiring to rise to power soon.

SIZING UP AN OPPONENT'S STRENGTHS AND WEAKNESSES

Am I not destroying my enemies when I make friends of them?

Abraham Lincoln

Study your potential enemies' strategies; understand their trends and probable behavior. One of the chief tenants of Sun Tzu, the master Chinese general and strategist, is "Know your enemy as you know yourself and you will always be victorious." This premise is especially true in the semideadly world of office politics—where the ones you may be competing with will at some point face off against you either directly or indirectly.

In understanding your enemies, there are things that help you size them up. Some points have more weight than others, but this varies widely depending on your organization as well as the enemies you face and the stakes up for grabs. Each of these should be seen as measures of what makes your enemy (or potential enemy) strong or weak. They are factors worthy of consideration when it comes to dealing with those in your career who may undertake politics either for or against you.

While past behavior never is a perfect measure of what an individual will do in the future, it is the best reference that you are likely to be able to obtain given the nonstatic resources of the modern corporation.

Willingness to Take Risks

The amount of risk that people are willing to take is a measure of their character. It often reveals how they will act in the future—this is especially true in the world of office politics.

In many ways office politics is akin to poker. There is an ante, a minimum amount of risk that everyone is required to take just to play the game. As the game progresses, wagers are made. These risks, sometimes tangible, are the chips of power that players are willing to forfeit should they lose.

When looking to size up the strengths and weaknesses of your political enemies, evaluate what they are willing to risk. Are they small bidders, willing to take only small risks to get ahead, slowly and methodically gaining power? Or is your enemy willing to take large career risks?

Usually this can be best determined by looking at your enemies' career history. Those who show a series of promotions or advancements in power (more than three) usually take much smaller risks. They are in the proverbial game of politics for the long haul, willing to avoid large risks and instead to play many small political games and angles to get ahead.

Far more dangerous and unpredictable are those individuals who risk everything when waging political warfare. These individuals usually have meteoric careers, rising rapidly—often up several levels at a time. Risk takers of this type are dangerous because they are difficult to track in terms of what they are going to do next—their plans are often so bold and daring that the scale is hard to imagine.

Rapidity of Action

When viewing your potential political foes, another critical factor is the span of time between their political acts. Some individuals only dabble in office politics, enough to keep their careers afloat or salvageable. Others almost always have some act of politics in motion, maybe more than one.

What is more dangerous? The rapidity factor alone does not determine the danger level. However, from a predictability standpoint, it is much easier to deal with someone who is always embroiled in politics since the motivations are more blatant. Those who only occasionally take part in politics are nearly impossible to predict unless there is some sort of pattern in what causes them to take part. For example, if someone seems to play politics only when there is a reorganization in the works, you can bet that during the next reorganization, the dabbler will be out and about again.

Strategic Sense

In more common terms, this is an evaluation of your enemies in terms of long-range thinking. Are they working toward an obvious career goal and taking the logical steps necessary to get to that position? This is an indication of strategic thinking, and therefore of a person who is a dangerous threat in terms of potential political action. Individuals who are obviously pursuing long-range plans and goals should be seen as a greater risk to you as you enter or attempt to survive politics. Since they integrate their actions as part of a broader plan, their very nature makes them dangerous in encounters where power is at stake.

The opposite of a strategic thinker is a reactionary individual. Rather than mapping out a long-term plan, this individual exploits, acting only when forced to or out of survival necessity. Tracking political opponents of this type is an effort of evaluating what criteria set them off, that is, what triggers their participation in politics? Is it annually during promotion announcements? Is it just prior to performance reviews? Or is it when the Dow Jones plummets more than 40 points in a day? Knowing what the triggers are gives you advance knowledge as to when the nonstrategic thinkers will act—in essence giving you power of control over the situation . . . especially if their actions are predictable.

Self-Restraint

Perhaps one of the most telling measures of a political opponent is to know how far down your opposition will stoop to achieve victory. Is he willing to crush other individuals' careers, or is he only willing to injure reputations in the quest for power?

This is an important factor to gauge your potential opposition—it tells you what he may be willing to do to you should he face you one day squarely in political combat. This is the bloodthirstiness factor. This determines if your opponent has a killer instinct or likes playing with victims just to soften them up.

A way to approach this is to ask where the skeletons are buried. Everyone involved in internal politics is going to have people they have crossed either directly or indirectly in their careers. Knowing what became of the victims gives you insights as to the bloodthirstiness of your foe. If the opposition in the past has been merely demoted or transferred, then you are facing a more humane, less cutthroat opponent. On the other hand, if you discover that your foe has argued a previous rival into a stroke over a conference table, you know are dealing with someone who has tasted blood and savors it.

Flexibility

The modern office is one of constant change. As a result, your own plans will need to be flexible to be effective. The same can be said for those of your opponents. As you take a look at their track records, the aspect of *flexibility* becomes critical to evaluate, even if you are trying to avoid taking part in politics. Has your future foe been close to dealing with a losing situation and managed to turn it around? Do your sources indicate that your foe is able to make up the plans necessary for politics on the fly, constantly adapting and changing to the opposition? If so, you are dealing with a potential foe who is most dangerous.

If not, you may be dealing with an anal-retentive individual who locks onto a mode of operation and sticks with it. This is known as Titanic Syndrome. Much like the captain of the *Titanic,* despite warnings and common sense, the individual plows straight ahead and often into deeper disaster. This trait and way of thinking tells you that you can force this opponent into a course of action and that once it's started, it will rapidly become inescapable.

Sacred Ground

Survival in internal office politics is not something that takes place in a vacuum. Everyone who aspires to power uses something as a source of power or has something they will not organize against. It may be a person that the politician respects too much to move against or, more often, someone with information (dirt) on the politician.

Who do your potential enemies distance themselves from? Who won't they touch in their devious plans for power? Have they had opportunity to strike at someone or some department and passed up on it?

Once you learn what is sacred to a potential foe, it represents a potential target. This may be your foe's biggest backer, a source of power in the organization. Knowing this provides you with a better understanding of where your likely enemy will not strike. It also provides you the necessary insight as to whom, if you were to involve yourself in politics, you are most likely going to have to move against.

If you are a person who does not want to take part in office political infighting, knowing the sacred spots will often give you a less turbulent working environment. Report to that person or work in that department, and you may be less in the line of fire than in other places of your company or firm.

Motivation: Ego or Career

Power is most often the bait that lures individuals into taking part in office politics. Assumption or usurpation of power is done for one of two reasons. One is to satisfy a career goal, the other is to fulfill one's ego. Understanding which of these two factors motivates your potential foe is important—it defines how far the target politician is willing to stoop.

This is not to say that one reason is more common than the other. Both reasons are common and vary by organization and individuals involved. What is important is that individuals who seek to advance their career for the sake of where they fit in an organization are oftentimes less willing to take extreme risks. They concentrate solely on their image and posture in the workplace and take part in political actions aimed at defining the course of their careers. To them, the workplace is the limit of where they look. The politics they involve themselves with is limited to the office.

The opposite is true of those individuals who are motivated to satisfy their personal egos. They are more dangerous to deal with—to them, everything is fair game when taking part in politics. They are willing to strike at people's personal lives, families, and so on. They see no bounds in just dealing with the office as the environment where they wage their backstabbing efforts. To them, crushing an enemy may mean breaking up a marriage, exposing a child's drug or drinking problem, locating and distributing those embarrassing (and compromising) photos from the Christmas party five years ago—anything goes.

I'm proud that I'm a politician. A politician is a man who understands government, and it takes a politician to run a government.
A statesman is a politician who's been dead 10 or 15 years.

Harry S. Truman

MARKING
YOUR TERRITORY

So far, we've defined politics, determined your potential for being exposed to the people who take part in politics, and decided who may stand out as an enemy. Now it's time for self-reflection. In other words, How political am I? What is my potential to take on the rest of the office in a bloodfest for power and prestige? What kind of cubicle warrior am I?

SELF-ANALYSIS

This is a questionnaire aimed at helping you determine what role you are most likely to take in corporate politics. It is not scientific by any stretch of the imagination. Instead, it poses real-world questions to elicit answers as you might respond in your current workplace.

To make full use of the self-analysis you need to answer the questions and total your score. At the end of the questionnaire, the questions are broken down to provide you a means of determining what degree, level, and severity of political action you are most comfortable with.

Instructions

Answer each of the questions by selecting the number that most accurately reflects how you would react to the situation in your current job or in the situation described. Under each question is a description of what selecting each option represents. Option #1 is always the least political response and #10 the most political, with #5 being the middle ground.

You will notice a *W, B,* or *D* beside the number for each question. Ignore these for the moment; they classify the questions and contribute to the end analysis of your political potential. When you total your score on the test, you will not just total your overall rating points but will subtotal for each of these three factors.

The first question asks about cheating on tests. Here's how to place your response: If you normally wouldn't cheat on a test but might be willing to if the circumstances were just right, you might select #4 or #5. If you assuredly would cheat but probably wouldn't be willing to frame another student in the process, you might select #8 or #9 depending on how extreme your feelings are.

1W. Would you cheat on a test that you knew you were going to otherwise fail, if you knew that you stood no chance of being caught?

1   Never. Cheating is unethical.

2

3

4

5   I would cheat if I knew for sure that I could get away with it.

6

7

8

9

10 Not only would I cheat, but I would inform the instructor that the person I copied from cheated off of me!

2W. Percentage of waking hours you spend working or thinking about work each week? *Note: A typical week of 40 hours (like anyone out there still manages to work only 40 hours) would take up approximately 23 percent of your waking time, assuming you never think about work off the job.*

1   20% or less

2   25%

3   30%

4   35%

5   40%

6   50%

7   60%

8   70%

9   80%

10 90% or more

3W. Indicate the percentage of time you spend socializing in the workplace. *This is defined as time you spend discussing work, fellow employees, last night's TV, and so on, but not actively conducting business operations assigned to you.*

1   0

2   5% or less

3   6%–10%

4   11%–20%

5   21%–30%
6   31%–40%
7   41%–45%
8   46%–50%
9   51%–55%
10   56% or more

4B. A project you were working on with others has been declared a failure by management. You are more likely to:

1   Accept responsibility for the failure and problems and get on with life.

2

3

4

5   Maintain a low profile and hope that you will not be implicated in the failure.

6

7

8

9

10 Actively point out to management who was responsible for the project falling apart (whether they were guilty or not).

5W. You see an opportunity to work with someone management regards as a "rising star" on a new project. Your reaction typically would be:

1   Take no action. If they want me to work on the job, management will let me know.

2

3

4

5   Drop appropriate hints with the right people to let them know that I am interested in the project.

6

7

8

9

10 Actively seek out a position on the project, even to the point of undermining others who might be vying for the same position.

6D. In preparing a budget, how much would you be willing to pad—that is, overestimate—it for management?

1 None. I have a responsibility to the company to report the figures to the best of my ability.

2 5% or less

3 6%–10%

4 11%–15%

5 16%–20%

6 21%–25%

7 26%–30%

8 31%–40%

9 41%–59%

10 I like to think of a budget as a rough guideline. I usually pad it by 60% or more. That way I can almost always be assured of coming in under budget!

7B. A co-worker confides some personal information that indicates the company or firm has lost a great deal of money due to the co-worker's mismanagement. Both of you are up for a promotion and there are limited number of promotions this year. Your typical response to this situation would be:

1 Take no action since I believe in being promoted on my merits, not because of the failings of others.

2

3

4

5 Reveal the information if my manager asks me, otherwise keep it to myself.

6

7

8

9

10   Use the information that my co-worker gave me to ensure that I obtain the promotion.

8W. Number of bits of unconfirmed information (rumors) that you pass on in a given week.

1   None. Gossip has no place in the office.

2   1

3   2

4   3

5   4

6   5

7   6

8   7

9   8

10   I pass on almost every rumor in some way, just to stay in touch with the grapevine.

9B. You are standing at a network printer or fax waiting for your information when you notice several faxes or pages that belong to your boss regarding your project. You would most likely:

1   Divert my eyes or flip the information over so I could not read it.

2

3

4

5   Casually glance at the material.

6

7

8

9

10   Make copies of the information if possible. If not, at least read all of it.

10W. A competing manager asked to meet with you. On the way there, you spot the manager in a meeting that you know will run for another half hour at least. You show up at the manager's office and find it empty, the terminal logged in and the manager's e-mail up on the screen in plain view. If you close the door, you know you could read it without being seen. You would:

1   Not pay attention to it. The information is private and not for my attention.

2

3

4

5   Glance at it to see if it was of interest and read anything I could get at casually.

6

7

8

9

10   Check the e-mail. Forward those messages that seem to be of interest to my own e-mail account.

11W. Number of communications (voice mail or e-mail messages and so on) you send out per week to cover yourself (that is, to simply put in writing or confirm information so that you will be protected in the future):

1   None. Our office operates on trust.

2   1

3   2–3

4   4–5

5   6–7   In terms of e-mail I often print or store these messages in case I need to verify or defend myself in the future.

6   8

7   9

8   10–12

9   13–15

10   16 or more

12W. Number of meetings, conference calls, or VTCs (video teleconferences) that you attend in a typical week:

1   One or none. Most of my time is spent doing my job.

2   2

3   3

4   4

5   5

6   6

7   7

8   8

9   9–10

10   11 or more. The vast majority of my time is spent in meetings or conference calls.

13W. The number of committees, groups, project teams, and so on, that you are currently assigned to. *Note: For each one that you chair, add two to the number.*

1   None

2   1

3   2

4   3

5   4

6   5

7   6

8   7

9   8

10   9 or more

14B. One of your colleagues has been laid off and has been escorted from the building with his personal possessions. His office is isolated and you can access it without being seen. What best describes your actions:

1   I would do nothing. This is not my concern.

2

3

4

5   I would casually go in and take office supplies—but only if other employees had done it before me and it was known.

6

7

8

9

10 I would actively loot the desk. Priorities would be to obtain any
and all files or work information that would assist me in my job.

15B. Your periodic report to management has information in
it that may indicate that you are not managing the project to the best interests of the company or firm. Your reaction would be to do the following:

1 Report the information factually. Let the chips fall where they may.

2

3

4

5 Conceal the information that might damage me. In fact, I would
attempt to cover myself in the report—including a "slight adjust-
ment" of the information.

6

7

8

9

10 Use the report to deflect the damage to me. I would try to name a
possible scapegoat for the shortcomings. If necessary, I would actively falsify information to protect my career.

16W. What is the number of meetings, communications, and
calls per week you have with your direct manager's
manager or anyone else above your boss in the organization chart:

1 None. I never meet my boss's boss or any of upper management.
Nor do I send them reports, e-mail, or anything else.

2 1

3 2

4 3

5 4 Most of these meetings are informal and I almost always pass
on information about these meetings to my manager.

6 5

7 6

8 7

9   8

10   9 or more. I regularly am in communication with management
     above my own supervisor and do not reveal the contents of those
     meetings or even that they take place.

17D. You have a project that has come apart at the seams. One
of the team members is politically weak and could easily
be implicated as the individual responsible for the failure. Your typical action given these circumstances is:

1   I would do nothing. Everyone on the team bears some responsibil-
     ity for the project's failure.

2

3

4

5   I am more than willing to take my blame, but if possible I will de-
     flect as much of the responsibility to this person.

6

7

8

9

10   I would covertly shuffle as much blame as possible to the obvious
     victim. When somebody is carrying a big, flashing sign saying
     "scapegoat," why should my career suffer?

18D. One of your staff was up for a promotion but you did not
fight hard enough to secure it. When you meet with that
person in performance reviews, you will most likely:

1   Accept the blame and say that I should have fought harder for the
     promotion.

2

3

4

5   Be evasive about the reason the promotion didn't come through. I
     might go so far as to hint that upper management simply didn't
     support it.

6

7

8

9

10   Blame a competing manager, lie about the number of promotions available, or even blame my boss rather than let anyone know it was all my fault. The last thing I would ever do is let my staff think I let them down.

19D. You pass a couple of managers at the same level as your own supervisor in the hall and overhear their conversation. One of them mentions your boss's name and some trouble that is brewing. You gather enough information without them knowing to tip off your boss to the potential threat. Your typical action would be to:

1   Do nothing. This is rumor information and none of my business at best.

2

3

4

5   Pass the information on to my supervisor privately. Protecting my manager is important to me.

6

7

8

9

10   Contact the manager who was speaking in the hall and hint that I have information to support the issue and would be willing to provide it—in the spirit of cooperation.

20D. You have a chance to take a position in the company on a high-profile project. This means giving up your secure job and making a lateral move. The manager of the new project is a rising star in the company and the project has strong backing, but if it fails, you may find yourself unemployed. Given these circumstances you:

1   Remain at my present job. For a lateral move, the risks are too great.

2

3

4

    5   Consider making the move as long as I manage to maintain a toe-hold in my present job in case things don't turn out so well on the new project.

    6

    7

    8

    9

   10   Leap at the chance. This might allow better positioning for future jobs. If nothing else I can ride this project manager's coattails on the way up.

21D. At the next level of management above you there are four managers all vying for position and waging cubicle warfare with each other at will. You want to climb up, but the minute they realize you have such an interest, you know it will cause them to come after you as a potential threat. Given this information you:

    1   Take no action. It is best to let them fight it out and then align myself with whoever wins.

    2

    3

    4

    5   Work covertly to position myself for promotion. Keep as low a profile as possible so as to not attract their attention or wrath.

    6

    7

    8

    9

   10   Play them against each other while at the same time painting myself as "apolitical" with their boss—the best candidate to be in charge of them once their infighting settles.

22B. You are trying to expedite the purchase of some computer hardware but the purchasing agent for your company or firm has stalled it for so-called technical reasons. The agent does not return your phone calls and when you lost your temper a week ago, you got the impression that your order went to the bottom of the pile. Your response would be to:

1 Call the agent and apologize. Try to appeal to human kindness.

2

3

4

5 Go over the little toad's head to the next manager up.

6

7

8

9

10 Drop a hint with Human Resources and even the Purchasing VP that you've heard that the agent has been getting kickbacks from several vendors. (After all, the agent they hire after they fire this one may be more reasonable.)

23D. Upper management has announced a companywide downsizing and reorganization. Many of your peers are afraid they will lose their jobs as a result. Your course of action would be to:

1 Remain calm. There's nothing I can do about it anyway. I'll opt to ride out the storm.

2

3

4

5 Do what I can to increase my group or team's productivity. Expand my communications so that upper management sees that I am a real go-getter.

6

7

8

9

10 Draft my own copies of how I'd reorganize things (keeping myself on the org charts of course). I'd send these to my manager's boss, if not higher.

24D. The position you envision yourself being in within the next 5 to 10 years is:

  1 My manager's or supervisor's job.

  2

  3

  4

  5 At least two more levels up the management food chain, essentially being at the level of my boss's boss.

  6

  7

  8

  9

 10 At least four levels higher in the company or firm or the highest position possible. A vice president, partner, or higher level, no matter what the body count has to be to get there.

25B. The number of people who have been fired, driven into retirement, or forced to resign after your direct input into the decision. This includes staff reporting directly to you whom you have had to fire.

  1 None

  2 1

  3 2

  4 3

  5 4

  6 5

  7 6

  8 7

  9 8

 10 9 or more. In fact, I may have been involved in decisions to out-source entire departments or groups, or to sell entire divisions of our company.

26D. A fellow manager who has been a rival in the past suggests that the two of you work together on a project. There is some risk involved in the project and in the past you know that this individual has attempted to assassinate your character with upper management, but the offer seems genuine and sincere and would offer you a chance to achieve more recognition and greater power or prestige. Knowing this you would:

1   Accept the offer and hope that the experiences we've had in the past are now behind us.

2

3

4

5   Let the opportunity go. This manager can't be trusted—and clearly needs me more than I need the headaches.

6

7

8

9

10 Accept the offer and approach my new posting cautiously. If I got the chance, I'd pay this manager back for past actions.

27B. The project you're on is falling apart due to high personnel turnover and lack of support from your management. Its failure could damage your long-term career prospects. Your reaction to this would be to:

1   Report the problems to my supervisor and attempt to elicit some support in managing the project.

2

3

4

5   Reorganize the project staff. I would motivate what personnel are left.

6

7

8

9

10 Get off the project and make sure that someone—even my manager—is set up as the appropriate scapegoat for the failings.

Overall Scoring: Your Strengths and Weaknesses

Total up your score. For each question type (W, B, or D) total what their independent scores are.

Total Score_____   Total W_____   Total B_____   Total D_____

The rankings in Table 3.1 indicate, based on your total score, the school of political thought that you most likely subscribe to.

TABLE 3.1.   Political Positioning Table.

Score:	Political Positioning or School of Thought:
27–70	*Politically Naïve.* With this ranking, you are a person who believes that good things come to those who wait. (According to some, you still believe in the Tooth Fairy, Santa Claus, and a strong Democratic president.) You place ethics and morality above all. In many cases you are the victim of politics but never initiate action on your own.
71–125	*Politically Challenged or Reactionary.* In your mind, politics is something that is to be dabbled in only when it is necessary. There are times that you believe in taking a political role, but usually in response to some external stimulus or someone else's political activity.
126–185	*Politically Active.* Whether you've actively thought about it or not, you take part in office politics often enough to have your name known in such circles. You tend to use politics when you can exploit the situation, but rarely do you use it to manipulate your career.
186–200	*Politically Ambitious.* You have your eyes on advancement and promotion, and you've tasted power and like the flavor. You tend to work in smaller plots and more in the open than some individuals, but you have had success in the past with politics and are willing to jump into the political pool at any given opportunity.
201+	*Strategically Aggressive.* You spend as much time playing politics as you do working.

Willingness   The total rating you have of questions listed with a *W* indicates your willingness to take part in politics. Moreover, it represents the temptations of politics inherent around you in your job—these temptations leading to political activity. Willingness represents opportunity and your own nature to take part in those opportunities.

Ratings under willingness can be interpreted as shown in Table 3.2.

TABLE 3.2.   Willingness Table.

Rating:	Level of Willingness:
10–40	*Environmental Willingness.* Where you currently work in your company or firm has little potential for allowing you the opportunity to take part in politics, and even when it does, you do not take part unless forced to.
41–70	*Opportunist.* You do not see yourself as willing to take part in politics, but will do so when there are motivating factors that appeal to you.
71+	*Political Animal.* You cannot pass up the chance to indulge yourself in politics. You are hooked, an addict. Given the least opportunity, you will take advantage of your political skills and apply them.

Bloodthirstiness   When taking an active role in politics, you will engage others, and the costs may be their careers and livelihoods—or your own. Even if you are not seeking to be politically active, there is a line that has to be drawn where you make a stand or perish.

The rating in Table 3.3 describes your willingness to draw political blood. Just how far will you go? What is the limit that you are going to press in a situation?

TABLE 3.3. Bloodthirstiness Table.

Rating:	Level of Bloodthirstiness:
8–12	*Wuss.* If politics were a sport, you'd prefer golf. You'll take part in politics, but not if it involves risking your career or someone else's.
13–60	*Fencer.* You take the risks and pay the price when it comes to political endeavors. In your mind there are rules to be followed and when it comes to going for the proverbial kill, you always weigh that against the benefits and risk. You are willing to take out an opponent, but the rewards have to be right for you—and substantial.
61+	*Killer.* The odds do not drive your willingness to enter a fight and take out an enemy. You always fight to the finish, always throw the last blow.

Depth The questions that center on depth are those that look at your long-range planning. Political connoisseurs of merit do not live for tomorrow; they weave plots and plans that will advance them in the far future.

TABLE 3.4. Depth Table.

Rating:	Level of Depth:
9–14	*Tactical Thinker.* The extent of your thinking is not far beyond your next meal, let alone on your career future. You tend to take advantage of politics, but your planning is limited to the project that you are currently working on, not how this plan fits into a larger picture.
15–65	*Lieutenant General.* You have some vague long-range plans for where you think your career is going. When you do take part in politics, you generally try and fit the effort into your long-range vision. There are times you wander from this, but for the most part you always try to keep your career goals focused.
66+	*Strategic Thinker.* Your plans are all part of a greater scheme, one that you control. Every political ploy you hatch is part of a greater master plan that you control and contort in your own image. You see threats in the here and now and squash them only if they pose a threat to your greater future.

Table 3.4 is a breakdown of how you rate in terms of strategic planning and thinking.

THE LIFE CYCLE OF THE CUBICLE WARRIOR

The life cycle of politics (a.k.a. the life cycle of the cubicle warrior) shown in Figure 3.1 is the cycle that an individual goes through in an organization from the first day on the job to the last. Understanding where you are in your life cycle is important in that it often may assist you in explaining why you rated the way you did in the self-assessment. It also provides some insight as to what your political future may be, even if you do not want to take an active role in office politics.

Every manager goes through this life cycle in some way. What varies from individual to individual is how long a person spends in each of the phases.

FIGURE 3.1.   Cubicle Warrior Life Cycle.

Adjustment Period

This occurs early in your career in an office or organization. It is the time when you are learning the limitations of your company or firm, the norms of acceptable behavior, and who is in power. This orientation period may last anywhere from your first week on the job to your first year.

During this period your activities in office politics are limited, mostly because you are not sure of your environment or what the expectations are. Likewise you do not know how your management will react. If you are in this phase of your career with a company or firm, your Bloodthirstiness score is generally lower as is your Depth since you have not had time to lay out long-range plans and are still attempting to figure out who the political players are.

Positioning Phase

During this phase you have a firm understanding of the company norms and accepted behavior. You have managed to digest where the power is located, determine who has it, and understand the history of politics in your organization (what works and what does not). When in the Positioning Phase, you begin the process of laying out your long-range plans as well as aligning yourself with the right individuals to get ahead.

In the Positioning Phase, your Bloodthirstiness score is low but your Willingness to take part in politics begins to rise (should you opt to take part in politics at all). Your Depth ratings will rise as you begin to sculpt out career paths and plans to undertake to advance your career.

Aggressive Phase

In the Aggressive Phase, if you are political or taking part in office politics, you are actively executing plans, implementing strategies and tactics, and so on to get ahead. If you are the kind of person who does not want to take part in politics, you are aggressively fending off attacks and maintaining your position as a nonpolitical player.

In the midst of this phase, all three ratings are likely to be elevated (Bloodthirstiness, Willingness, and Depth) as you launch assaults, brownnose, and otherwise wield your political sword in battle. Willingness can waver depending on your successes, with failures often making individuals draw back from political activities.

Defensive Posturing Phase

The problem with power is that once you have it, you must defend it. This is known as the Defensive Posturing Phase. Having achieved some degree of success in your long- and short-term plans, you now enter a phase of your career where you must fend off assaults by those who are out to strip you of your power.

It is here that Bloodthirstiness reaches its pinnacle. Your Willingness rating will most likely plateau as you become selective in picking the battles you intend to fight. Depth also diminishes since, if you've done everything right, you are at the peak of your game and position within the organization.

YOUR DEN OF POWER: YOUR OFFICE

Every cubicle warrior needs a place to recoup, rebuild, and plan the next assault. This is your bunker. It is where plans are made and deals are sealed. In other words, it's your office.

An office is a reflection of your management style. It is an extension of yourself, it stands as a symbol of you even when you are not there. It is similar to the royal audience chambers of kingdoms past; places where the kings and queens met the lesser lords of the realm and where edicts became the law of the land.

If you are involved with politics, how your office is outfitted and equipped not only enhances your reputation but your power as well. The items listed here are what the top-of-the-line office politics maven is apt to want, and should give you insights as to how to equip your own office as well.

amous Political Players of the Past History is laden with names of people who stood out for one reason or another as political figures. This is not to say that these individuals are all to be admired and copied, but they do represent a cross-section of people who manipulated the office politics of their day.

Cain Depending on your beliefs and interpretation of the Bible, Cain stands out as one of mankind's earliest recorded figures who took politics into his own hands. While jealousy is seen as his primary driving factor for killing his brother Able, the underlying truth is that with the death of Able, Cain figured his position as favorite son would be ensured for all time.

Brutus As a Roman senator, Brutus realized that his career was only hindered by his manager—Caesar. Regardless of your opinion of his technique, Brutus managed to organize an internal office coup d'état with eleven other senators (no small task given the maze of Roman politics at the time) and showed a high level of bloodthirstiness in dealing with Caesar—killing him publicly certainly solved the immediate problem.

Attila the Hun To add some perspective, the tribes of Huns were disorganized raiding nomads for generations. Attila was captured by the Romans and was raised as a "friendly hostage" in Rome, where he developed contempt for his captors. It was custom for the Romans to hold young nobles as hostages, a policy of keeping enemies close at hand and holding their homelands in check since the heirs were in their enemies' hands.

When he assumed the leadership of the Huns, Attila organized them as a single people, straightened out their priorities, and executed plans he had laid out as a captive to sack the very empire that had held him hostage. His strategic thinking stands out as an example for office managers everywhere.

Benedict Arnold   Benedict Arnold was not a grandly successful political player, but his case stands out as one worth evaluating nevertheless. A patriot and business-man during the American Revolution, he proved himself as a skilled military tactician. His political skills lacked, however. His loans to the Colonial Congress went unpaid and his business ventures suffered greatly from the lack of funds he had been promised and denied.

Arnold was not fighting the war for glory, but for profit—something to warm the cockles of any red-blooded entrepreneur's heart. When the congress denied repayment of his loans, he took a step that earned him a footnote in history; he planned to rebel and turn over West Point to the British.

Exposed as a traitor, Arnold got the power and position he sought as a general in the British Army, eventually fighting the Americans in Virginia two years after his be-trayal. He profited well in the short term from his defec-tion, even though West Point did not fall to the British. While he died poor, Arnold should be respected in office political circles for taking grand risks that others would never have considered.

Napoléon Bonaparte   From a practical and summarized standpoint, Napoléon is an example of political survival. He

continued

continued

took over a turbulent nation where power rose and fell like the tides. In his rise, he managed to navigate not just the military but a cumbersome national administrative machine. His success led to France controlling most of Europe.

Napoléon was eventually deposed and sent into exile, written off by his contemporaries. But even in exile he managed to stage a daring escape and return to power, once again embroiling Europe in war.

What makes Napoléon stand out is his sheer resilience and determination. Those who opposed him were done away with, buried, and swiftly forgotten. He quelled his competition and even in defeat, he managed to resurge to a near victory.

Dwight Eisenhower   The American military machine of the 1920s to the 1940s was a powder keg of egos and personalities all attempting to seize power and positions of prestige. Dwight Eisenhower managed to navigate these waters very carefully and successfully. At one point he was an assistant to another political powerhouse, General Douglas MacArthur . . . a role that some thought would cast him in a secondary position for the rest of his career.

It was not meant to be. Eisenhower managed not only to survive working for prima donnas, but he eventually ended up being commander of the Allied forces in Europe . . . essentially becoming the manager of most of the biggest egos in the civilized world. And after that, he was able to carry his career further to become president of the United States.

Lee Iacocca   This cigar-smoking businessman beat incredible odds to rise to the pinnacle of success at Chrysler.

He began as a car salesman in Pennsylvania and rose through the myriad corridors of power and politics at Ford Motor Company. Despite his successes, his clashes with the Ford family and with other managers cost him his job.

Iacocca should have been dead and buried in terms of auto-industry politics, but he managed to get into the then-suffering Chrysler Corporation's top slot. The company was in a shambles, but Iacocca moved at a speed that shocked the Big Three. Instead of trying to move the old cronies who had built empires in Chrysler, he shattered their holdings and power bases almost overnight, sending many old-dog managers into retirement. His unpublicized raids of key management staff at Ford were the stuff of legends in Detroit through the '80s, plucking them out of key projects with the lure of cash and power—often crippling Ford projects at the same time.

Richard Nixon   The career of Richard Nixon is a study of office politics carried out to the nth degree. Nixon understood the value of fear and leveraged it during the "Red scare" days of the post–World War II era to eventually become vice president of the United States. In his first bid for the presidency he lost out to John Kennedy and, like many of his great historical forebears, he should have been finished at that point. After that failure he even lost a gubernatorial bid.

Nixon understood his failures, learned from them, and overcame most of them. His presentation and appearance during the debates with Kennedy and his ongoing clashes with the press taught him the need to improve his control over communication. He stuck to simple issues, and when

continued

continued

the time came, the man most people had written off as politically buried emerged as a strong president.

The failures of Watergate are seen as his downfall, but if anything, they offer a glimpse into office politics on a grand scale that is worth evaluating. Richard Nixon was not a victim of shortsightedness—his history shows him to have been a strategic thinker. Instead, he failed to maintain a firm enough control over his staff.

Required Books

Silent Coup, Len Colodny and Robert Gettlin (to send fear into your own managers who visit).

The Prince, Niccolò Machiavelli (as the bible of departmental management).

The Art of War, Sun Tzu (to let visitors know that you are serious).

The Warren Commission Report (Hard Cover Summarized). Just to let people know that you are willing to go to extremes to get ahead.

Essential Stuff

A hollowed-out book: You need at least one for storing personal items or documents.

Private fax machine, copier, and printer: Why print on the network where anyone can read it? It's best to keep this stuff local.

Again America wrote off Nixon, but this too was a mistake. After spending a while in exile, Richard Nixon became a highly sought-after consultant on world affairs. Even near the time of his death he was a visitor at the Clinton White House. His persistence and long-range thinking have earned him a greater place in history than most textbooks will grant.

Dagger-shaped letter opener: Let your visitors see this as a symbolic deadly implement.

Motion sensor device: Security is one thing. Security that you can control is another. A simple $30 motion sensor on your computer and keyboard can put out a squeal of 300 decibels if disturbed and really make an office spy's day.

Double-locked filing cabinet: The additional exterior lock is not just for visible deterrence but to augment the built-in devices so that no one would even consider trying to open them.

Bug detection device: These devices can be found in a number of catalogs and are useful for making sure that no one has bugged your office or is transmitting conversations during meetings. Hey, it's a dangerous world, why take chances?

Shredder: The only good documents are those that cannot be read by others. The true office politician never leaves a tangible audit trail. Nothing gets thrown away unshredded.

Retractable keyboard drawer: This allows you to lock up the keyboard all on its own, rendering access to your PC difficult at best.

Security cable: You can lose a lot if your hard drive walks out the door, so lock things down to make sure no one attempts a quick grab of your system.

Red-herring files and memos on desk: The cubicle warrior leaves nothing of importance on the desk or unsecured—period. The only things left out are red herrings: falsified memos, reports, graphs, and documents aimed at misleading anyone who would be willing to glance at them, even casually during a meeting. For real enjoyment, try out the ever-popular organization chart showing a vastly different reporting structure from the one in place.

Desktop items: These are items that bear the company or firm logo; your proof that you are a loyal employee—regardless of how many are actually items looted from the desks of former co-workers (possibly even people fired as a result of your actions). Paperweights, small clocks, chotchkes of all sorts on the desk and in the credenza show that you are one with the company.

A window: You've earned it by climbing on the backs of others.

Guest chairs: These should be lower than your own seat and as uncomfortable as possible. Your office is not for visitors to enjoy themselves. Instead it is a place where you want others to come in, see, respect, deposit information you can use, and leave.

Artwork on walls: As a demonstration of power, scenes of war are common. The American Civil War and the Napoleonic Wars are common. Sailing vessels are also important. These are not to relax your guests, but to make them understand that you respect power.

CD player with appropriate music selection: Military marches or classical music are most common. This is the music of power, timeless and dramatic. Nothing trendy or popular.

Stuff to Watch Out For

You wouldn't actually do anything illegal, of course, but the unscrupulous, hardball-playing political operative may well have some or all of these around the office:

Recording device: Usually concealed in a lockable drawer. Much like the devices in Nixon's Oval Office, these can be used to record conversations in the room.

Speaker phone with built-in recorder: Speaker phones are a politician's dream. You can never be sure who is in the room and listening to the conversation when speaking to someone on a speaker phone. Making it more appealing is the ability to tape the conversations for later use.

Concealed video camera: A number of security firms make video cameras that can be hidden in radios, clocks, or false books. These are very useful for taping meetings when audio alone won't suffice. After all, a picture is worth $1,000 or more in the right market. . . .

There is nothing more necessary than good intelligence to frustrate a
designing enemy, and nothing that requires greater pains to obtain.

George Washington

INTELLIGENCE GATHERING

A re you safe and secure in your office? Is anyone out there
reading your e-mail? Are your personal files safely locked
in your desk so that no one can get to them? To answer these
questions we must face the grim reality: nothing is totally secure,
and you have about as much privacy in the modern office as a
man standing at a urinal during a Yankees home game.

SPYING IN CORPORATE AMERICA

Corporate privacy and employee privacy are important issues in
the contemporary workplace, but their goals are often mutually
exclusive. The reason is simple: what you do on the job is considered property of the company or firm. As a result, managers
have unparalleled access to such things as long-distance phone

billings, e-mail traffic lists, and so on—information that protects the company and incidentally provides excellent material for blackmailing or monitoring and controlling the staff.

This is not a measure or question of ethics. In the blind, often mindless push of business toward a "paperless office" (something considered by most MIS managers as a sick and twisted pipe dream cooked up by an unnamed and often cursed middle-level manager), intelligence information often gets handed out freely. Adept cubicle warriors position themselves to get that information through legitimate means. And if that is not possible, aggressive political players take advantage of the weaknesses and flaws that are common in the systems and exploit them fully. Those who aim to carve out their careers through politics learn how to gain info through any and all means possible.

SURVEILLANCE IN THE OFFICE

Spying is such an ugly word. Let's use *intelligence gathering* or *surveillance* instead. Without information and intelligence, political aspirations and plans have no true substance. Intelligence information reveals what is happening, hints at what may happen in the future, and also exposes who the enemies are and what they are up to.

If information doesn't fall into their hands, politicos know that gathering it involves stealth, cunning, and a certain degree of pure guts, given the risks involved. In the sections that follow, you will read about the tips and methods that political heavy-hitters sometimes use to collect information. These examples illustrate the devious, low-down, and even illegal extremes that are possible in the real world. Become familiar with these methods and you will be better able to protect yourself and your data from office spies.

Hard Security

Hard security is the phrase often used for physical barriers. These are doors, windows, locking desks, filing cabinets, and so on. The phrase can also refer to any motion sensors or electronic devices that are used to secure doors or areas. Bottom line, it means anything that is protected by a physical lock or security device.

Novice spies—and novices at self-defense—often regard these as the most difficult barriers to circumvent. This is not necessarily the case. To be more accurate, this kind of security requires more advance planning to defeat, but there are many ways to beat it.

Obtaining Keys

One of the misconceptions most often perpetuated by facility managers is that it is next to impossible to get keys for locks (furniture, office, whatever). The truth of the matter is that it requires some creativity, but in many cases anyone can easily lay hands on such keys.

One of the more common methods is to require access due to project work hours. Depending on the type of work being done, employees sometimes need access to the office after hours—to upgrade computer systems when they're not being used for business, say, or to work late hours on a specific project or job. Outwardly demanding keys can be too blatant. Instead, the subtle office spy simply keeps requesting facility

ffice Spies: What They Look For   Office spies often have to wade through reams of paper or drawers of file folders in a short period of time, searching for useful information. You can make their lives difficult by keeping the most interesting stuff secure. Here's a typical spy's shopping list:

- *Proposed organization charts.* Oftentimes these provide glimpses into plans best kept private.
- *Budgets or actual expenditure reports.* These show where money is being spent, wisely or unwisely. Projected budgets show where money will be going, and what projects, plans, or staffing are most important.
- *Staffing plans.* Where there's headcount, there's political activity.
- *Anything marked "DRAFT."* These are usually things that have not been approved yet and may let an opponent get a jump start on you.

services or office services to grant access at odd hours. After enough times of having to come in at 2 A.M., the person stuck with the job will conclude that it is better to give the guy a personal set of keys rather than having to come in.

Several trends can work to a spy's advantage when it come to keys. First off, all the major furniture manufacturers usually key an entire desk set with the same key. In many cases, multiple copies of these keys are provided for the owner—usually one for each lock, which can add up to four or five keys, one of which may well be left lying around somewhere. The number imprinted on the keys and the name of manufacturer can also

- *Project plans and project flow charts.* These are critical since they reveal where each project's major milestone and potential stumbling block may be, allowing
  an opponent to formulate plans accordingly.
- *Personal calendars or day planners.* One, these can
  show your opposition who's meeting with you, allowing them to anticipate some of your moves. Two, they
  reveal when you're going on vacation, allowing the opposition to time their political advances for when you
  are weakest—when you are out of town.
- *Contracts or other legal documents.* If an opponent
  sees who you're dealing with and on what terms, he or
  she may move against your outsourced labor or firms,
  crippling you where you're weakest—in elements of
  the business that you don't control.

be useful. If a spy can appropriate one of the keys just long
enough to get the number, a note to the manufacturer claiming
to be the new facility or office manager may be enough to get a
duplicate key made. This does not work in all cases, of course,
but the security at most office furniture manufacturers tends
to be even more lax than it is around your average paper-
pushing offices.

Some people in the office really do need to have sets of keys
for everything. One of these is the office manager, another
might be the chief administrative assistant or secretary. Despite
all the layers of physical security that management might

ordain, a spy can often get hold of these keys once established as a friend and ally of the person in charge of them. The procedure is devastatingly simple. Whatever the falsified excuse, the spy's crucial ploy is to create a circumstance to *borrow* the keys—then scurry off to the key duplicating shop closest to the office, get a copy made ASAP, and get the keys back as quickly as possible. The key (pun boldly intended) is to return the master set in such record time that it seems impossible that anyone would have had enough time to make a new set.

It's also possible for a spy to get keys by simply stealing them and copying them. Copying them is important; the worst thing that anyone can do is to steal the keys and not return them. This attracts unwanted attention to the fact that the keys are out there somewhere, forcing management to change locks and maybe look for the culprit. However, if they disappear for only an hour or so, no one is likely to suspect that they have been duplicated.

Numeric Keypads

Someone came up with the concept of numeric locks with the hope that they would create a level of higher security. The truth of the matter is that these locks are even more susceptible to security breaches than normal key locks. What's the problem? The entire premise behind the security concept is that no one will share the code number, which is right up there with the premise that the Tooth Fairy makes office visits.

So where can a spy get the code? One way is to talk to former employees, especially those who might carry or bear a grudge against the company or firm. Usually the locks are not recoded after someone leaves, meaning that former employees often have codes—and are more than willing to share them.

Another method spies use is to watch someone entering and leaving the room. Keypads rarely use more than a three- or four-digit code. Someone who sees it done several times can easily figure out the combination and overcome the lock.

Another common method is to simply look at the keypad. The keys or the buttons that are most often used tend to be visibly worn. A three-digit code has so few possibilities that it's easy for a spy to break, given the right three buttons to work with. *Note: This method works only if the codes are not frequently changed, but few offices ever bother to change the codes. Make yours an exception!*

Electronically Locked Doors or Doors with Motion Sensors

Using electronic key locks, these doors usually have exterior keypads or lock systems to enter the building and a ceiling-mounted motion sensor to allow easy and fast exit. They usually use magnetic locks to keep the door from being easily opened. Bottom line, without the security key, magnetic card, or numeric pad code, nobody can open the door, right?

Not always true. The motion sensor tends to be the weakest link in the security chain. Sometimes spies can set it off by sliding several pieces of paper over the top of the door, allowing them to drift in front of the sensor—setting it off and thus unlocking the door.

Another method less commonly used involves a balloon. The would-be spy lies on the floor, inserts a balloon under the door, blows up the balloon as much as possible, and lets it go. As it deflates in the air, fluttering around, it can set off the motion sensor and pop the door open.

axims for Intelligence Gathering Getting caught in outright spying is one of the quickest ways to lose everything. Even the staunchest supporters will see too much political liability to stick by a captured spy. So here's what every spy lives by—and everyone else needs to watch out for:

- Never steal when you can copy. Stealing leaves too much of a trail that you've been there in the first place, and alerts people that their information may be known. Copy machines and cameras are the spy's best friends.
- Leave things exactly as you found them. If something is left a mess or out of place, it is the same as leaving a sign announcing that somebody was snooping.
- Always check the obvious first. Don't go looking for something to be hidden when it might be out in the open.
- Don't be obvious about the time you strike. If your building uses card security that can electronically track when you enter or leave, don't pick times to conduct

Electronic door systems are only as good as the updating of the security system behind them. In other words, when employees are terminated or lose their cards, make sure their access gets blocked. Most security systems claim this always gets done, but it's often not the case. When it fails, a spy can get a magnetic door card or the necessary code sequence from a former employee.

If all else fails, a really gutsy and dedicated spy may use the method known as *piggybacking*. This involves following someone in simply by coming up as the door opens. It's often possible for

your operations that stand out (say, 2:30 A.M.). Building security will check the anomalies in check-in and check-out times when something is reported stolen or missing.

■ Move quickly and quietly.

■ Prepare a cover story before you begin. If you get caught red-handed and try to fake your way out of an info-grab, you are most likely going to be dead meat. If you have a story worked out and rehearsed well in advance, however, you might just be able to bluff your way out.

The following is an example of how a bad cover story doesn't work: Francis Gary Powers (the U-2 reconnaissance pilot whose spy plane was shot down by the Russians, who captured and imprisoned him and milked the incident for all it was worth) gave the following statement upon his return to the United States: "I was a pilot flying an airplane and it just so happened that where I was flying made what I was doing spying." Not exactly the best cover ploy developed. . . .

the spy to walk right in, since people think it's rude to close the door in each others' faces and make their co-workers—even the ones they don't know by sight—go through the hassle of carding in. This is commonly done in many offices and no number of memos regarding security concerns stops the practice.

Up and Over

Most offices today have low-hanging drop ceilings to conceal the pipes and ducts and wiring that keep the building livable.

In many cases, the solid brick or wallboard walls do not go all the way to the next floor up. Instead, they stop just above the drop ceiling. So never assume a locked office is really locked. A spy with a ladder, some quiet time after hours, and a bit of upper body strength can push several of the ceiling tiles out of the way and climb into the drop ceiling and over most of the walls in the building—right down into an opponent's office, maybe yours.

"Bugs" Doesn't Necessarily Mean Roaches

The closed door and the sealed lips are prerequisites to tyranny.

Frank L. Stanton

Richard Nixon made the concept of taping conversations widely known—though the tapes had been rolling in the White House for several administrations before he came along. Not all surveillance need involve tape or video recording, however. In fact, some of the best information that can be gathered requires no more than listening in on conversations—an old and effective way to gain information and one that does not require hardware expertise to pull off. (More on this in the Eavesdropping section a bit later in the chapter.)

Getting back to recording, there are two kinds of conversations that a spy can tape or monitor: those where the spy is directly involved, which only borders on unethical behavior, and those where the spy is nowhere in sight—which jumps the line of ethical behavior as if it wasn't there at all. There are several ways to record first-person phone conversations. Many phone recording systems can do this easily, allowing the spy to walk away with a tape for later reviewing, blackmailing, or rear-end covering. Another popular method of executing this type of recording is to use the voice mail system. Several commercial systems can be set up to allow the recording of conversations.

Bugging or recording conversations not on a phone requires the spy to develop a little hardware skill and make a trip or two to the local Radio Shack or go through one of any number of electronics catalogs. Oddly enough, the devices needed to bug an office or conference room are relatively inexpensive to purchase—but more expensive ones are easier to hide. In some cases, a simple hand-held tape recorder will do the trick. Other situations may require radio microphones that can be concealed from view and set up to transmit to a recorder device.

Faxes and Network Printers

There are two resources that most people use around the office: network printers and fax machines. Both of these are excellent places to gather information and intelligence since any office is basically run on its paperwork. Careful loitering around fax machines and shared printers allows an intelligence gatherer to see what projects people are working on as well as what is being sent out for others to review.

An aggressive office politician can do more than simply lift copies of materials left mindlessly at these machines. Most laser printers have a hardware setting that allows someone to set how many copies of every document they print. Set it to two and there will always be a spare that can be taken quietly—either straight out of the hopper or from the recycling bin sitting beside the printer. (Some spies install their own recycling bins to make sure that individuals who realize they have two copies

ow Valid Is This Information? One of the primary questions you must ask about any information you gather—no matter how obscure—is, How valid or reliable is this? Without asking this question, you are liable to waste considerable time and resources on false leads, inaccurate information, or simple office gossip. Bottom line, do not act on information that you cannot verify.

How do you verify information? The most common method is corroboration—that is, does other information

will have a convenient place to put the second one (see the next section, Wastebaskets and Recycling Bins.)

Most fax machines also have the capability to print out a log of what calls and how many pages were sent from the machine as well how many pages came in and from what numbers. This information can reveal who is sending out résumés and where they're going, or if nothing else, where various individuals are sending information.

Wastebaskets and Recycling Bins

As stated before, the concept of a paperless office has been bandied about by many managers on the assumption that if a company uses less paper, it is somehow more efficient, its manager is more leaderlike, and its profitability will soar. This is roughly akin to the belief that if you stop smoking cigarettes the result will be world peace. As some long-lost sage once said, "We'll achieve a paperless office around the same time we achieve a paperless toilet."

support or substantiate it? You can extrapolate the information in terms of motives and results; that is, why would someone do or say this? What do they have to gain? Oftentimes picking apart the information leads to illogical conclusions that call the validity of the information into question.

Finally, there is the option of tracing the information to its source. In so doing, you often will learn where information may have become distorted, misquoted, or misunderstood. Was it a red herring on a fellow cubicle warrior's desk?

Most efforts to reduce paperwork simply generate more paper in both the long and short run. And the vast majority of paper created in the office ends up in wastebaskets or recycling bins. For a budding corporate intelligence officer, these repositories are excellent for finding hard copies of information—anything from performance reviews to project plans. The practice is commonly referred to as "dumpster diving" and is more often seen among younger staff members than older ones.

The best places to search are recycling bins since these are generally not tainted by liquids or leftover lunch. Other than that, the only thing dumpster divers have to do is time their raids on the trash so that they get it *after* the target leaves for the day and *before* the housekeeping staff shows up.

Eavesdropping

One of the oldest forms of corporate spying and intelligence gathering is simple eavesdropping, listening in on conversations you were not invited to take part in. This can be done in a number of different ways. In most offices with cubicles, listening in on those around you is far too simple . . . in fact, it's hard not to hear everything that goes on around you. As long as you don't look like you're listening in, people will assume that you are reading a report or working on something on your computer monitor, and you may overhear something juicy.

In enclosed offices, aggressive eavesdroppers sometimes take other measures. A common one is to adjust the ceiling tiles, offsetting one by a few inches. Lifting up a ceiling tile in an office or conference room allows sounds to travel upward. As much as 20 feet away, the spy can prop open another ceiling tile and listen in as long as no fire walls intervene between the target room and the listening post.

One factor that most office eavesdroppers fail to take into account is the fact that sound travels two ways. Remember, if you can hear someone, chances are they can hear you as well.

ELECTRONIC WARFARE

> The more you overthink the plumbing,
> the easier it is to stop up the drain.
>
> **Chief Engineer Montgomery Scott, *Star Trek III, The Search for Spock***

The blunt truth is that the automation of the office that took place across the corporate world in the 1980s and 1990s has forever changed the nature of political warfare and backstabbing. In the postwar years, information was limited to hard copy—paper. Now, with Local Area Networks, Wide Area Networks, e-mail, notebook computers with remote connectivity, the Internet, firewall security systems, and so on, information moves electronically through offices. Some pundits believe that a paperless society may emerge, but in reality many things still are printed and used as hard copy but are moved around the globe using electronics.

This changes the sophistication of someone attempting to get information. A higher level of computer savvy is required, as well as a stronger understanding of the principles, buzzwords, and protections that are in place.

Still, when all is said and done, everything comes down to a principle known as a password. Passwords are key words or phrases that allow you to feel that your data and information are secure.

Password Generation Schemes

Given this age of paranoia regarding security, the most common barrier is the password. A password is a written code that allegedly allows only the individual who creates it to get access to e-mail, computer networks, software applications, whatever the system owner wants to protect.

The truth of the matter is that most password generation schemes can be easily overcome by a person who wants to break into someone else's system or e-mail. To protect yourself, make sure that you do *not* use the common password formats discussed below. Most of the requisite information is readily accessible with only minimum research (thanks to the power of the Internet), meaning that anyone who wants to check out this information about somebody else stands a good chance of gaining access to whatever system the password is supposed to protect.

Most Common Passwords

- Names. (The user's full first or middle name, the spouse's or children's names, the individual's nickname, family dog's name, secretary's name, and so on.) Combinations of these names are commonplace—the wife's first name and the daughter's middle name, for example.
- Birthdays (personal, spouse, children, parents). *Note: People who think they're clever use combinations such as the user's birth month, the child's day, and the spouse's year.*
- Anniversary date (parents' or user's own).
- Phone number (home, childhood or parents' home, and so on).
- Address (house number or street name will do nicely, thank you).
- Zip code (number—current or childhood home number).
- Social security number.
- Year (birth, children's birth, parent's birth, and so on).
- College name or initials.
- Year of graduation from high school or college.
- The word *password*. (This comes installed with many systems, and the user is supposed to change it right away. It's the epitome of poor security and weak common sense to keep it, but many managers and employees do so—and even use it on other systems—because it is so easy to remember.)
- Car license plate number.
- QWERT. (Systems people understand this more than anyone else. It's the row of keyboard keys above the left hand—often chosen because it's easy to remember.)

Common Mistakes   The following tips will help you ensure your own privacy. They're the first things individuals seeking to penetrate system security will check out when gathering intelligence:

■ Any sticky note attached to a monitor may have the user's password on it.

■ The Rolodex, phone book, or some other visible and easily accessible record is a common spot to hide a password.

■ Anything visible in the office—a book title or author in plain sight, for example—or the name of a current or former project makes a nice, memorable password.

■ A secretary's workstation is apt to contain some sort of reference to the boss's password.

■ The computer software or hardware manual may mention the default installation password (probably "Password" as noted earlier). *Note: Users are expected to change this, but many will try to retain it. An MIS department that isn't properly organized or managed will let them get away with it.*

Good Password Generation Schemes How to protect yourself? First, pick a password that no one is likely to know or be able to figure out by accessing information regarding your life. Second, change your password often and regularly to prevent someone who gets access to it from getting much benefit. Third, never write down your password or give it to anyone.

Some suggestions:

■ The name of your favorite TV, motion picture, or literary character. *Note: Do not pick anything that is visible in your office.*

■ A work-related acronym that only you would know or understand. Example: MBIAM (My Boss Is A Moron).

■ Your enemies' names. (The last thing anyone would expect—unless they read this book!)

■ Titles of songs that you like.

■ A random number that only you know.

Nuked Till It Glows

Computer data is stored magnetically and thus is subject to the influence of other magnets. Simple common refrigerator magnets can destroy the data on a floppy diskette in a matter of seconds. For larger jobs such as hard drives, it takes something like a video-cassette eraser—essentially a large electromagnet. When turned on, it can fry the data on a hard drive in a matter of seconds and has a range of at least a foot.

Why would anyone destroy someone's data? Simply put, only a very small percentage of computer users maintain active backups of their data. One reason is that it is considered a waste of precious time in this age of hard drive reliability. Second, the backup diskettes and tapes become security risks on their own if they fall into the wrong hands. So the stuff on the hard drive is likely to be the only copy, and if it gets destroyed, it's probably gone for good—leaving the owner to spend time reconstructing it instead of engaging in more effective work or political maneuvering.

Can the data be recovered despite magnetic nuking? There are some sophisticated data recovery services that can, at a high price, recover data even from systems that have been submerged in salt water. The key is that these services cost large amounts of money and time, which can cripple a project. If you disdain politics, it is important to know that these services exist in case you are the victim of this form of corporate sabotage.

THE ROLE OF COUNTERINTELLIGENCE

The whole art of politics consists in directing
rationally the irrationalities of men.

Reinhold Niebuhr

It has often been said that the best defense is a good offense—
and the role of counterintelligence in office politics is to mislead your political opposition or those seeking to exploit the
knowledge you possess. This is a deliberate act on your part,
and one you need to consider whether you are merely trying to
survive the politics of your office or planning to take a more active role.

The centerpiece of office counterintelligence is the assumption that even if you are not waging political war, others are
doing so with you. In other words, assume that others in your
office are going through your trash, raiding your desk or office,
trying to access your e-mail account, and so on—whether or
not you have any evidence to that effect.

Even if you do not play office politics, you work for someone who works for someone else, and that means information
you have may be of some value to someone else in the company or firm. Or if you seek a political livelihood, take the
measures to make sure that your plans are not undone by weak
intelligence management on your part.

How do you react to this? Look at earlier sections of this
chapter and work accordingly. Don't leave your important papers out or sitting in the fax machine or copier. Change your
desk or office locks occasionally. Change your passwords often
and make them impossible to figure out. Always shred your
copies. In plain English, don't set yourself up to be a pawn

in someone else's political game by not managing your information.

Red Herrings Galore!

A red herring is a bit of false information planted with the aim of misleading the opposition or getting them to waste resources on fruitless efforts and pursuits. If you are a person with an active political life, remember that the use of red herrings is often what separates the novices from the masters. If you do not like the horrors of office politics, you can use red herrings to keep other political players at bay.

Red herrings can take many forms in the office. Memos (almost always labeled "Draft") are the most common, but people also falsify reports, fake performance reviews and proposed organizational charts and plans, or simply produce bogus proposals. What all red herrings have in common is that they have little bearing in reality. In fact, they are falsified in order to mislead anyone who reads them.

When putting together a red herring, make it as plausible and realistic as possible. Think of it like this—whoever reads it should believe that there is a sound business reason for it or that the herring has some basis in reality. It should be structured so that it is difficult to verify, referencing such high levels of management that no one would ever call to confirm, or people no longer employed by the company. Even better, create a memo or document (unsigned of course) as if it were written by someone else.

When you create your red herring, ask yourself a simple starter question: Will this implicate me or otherwise damage my career? If the answer is yes, then the red herring is not a good approach. If the answer is no, then move on to the next question: If this falls into the hands of others, will it damage them or cause them to waste time and effort? If the answer is no, once again the false information is no good. If the answer is yes, you have yourself a good example of the kind of rumor or misdirection that makes an excellent red herring.

The key element of any good red herring is the planting of it. Leaving it on your desk in plain view is not uncommon. If anyone is going through your papers, they are likely to find it. Printing it out and leaving it at the network printer or at a fax machine is a good way to make sure that the grapevine picks up on it as well. A red herring only begins to work when it is picked up and finds its way to the opposition.

ECM: Electronic Countermeasures

Electronic Countermeasures take several different forms in the office. One increasingly common form is antibugging devices—things that detect bugging devices or simply render them ineffective. The most simple of these are white-noise generators. These can be ordered from a surveillance catalog, but a common desk fan will often do the job. Running loud enough, it can generate background noise that drowns out many less expensive bugging devices.

Electronics, military surplus, and personal security stores and catalogs also provide a wide range of relatively inexpensive bug detection devices. These are hand-held and allow you to check an office to see if there are any active bugging devices in the room. These are the kinds of devices that you should only consider investing in if you are convinced that someone is monitoring discussions in your office or workspace.

Moles in Your Own Organization

The grim reality of corporate life often is that people in your group, team, or department are double agents . . . moles. They are passing information to your political foes and opposition. Whether they are doing this knowingly or inadvertently through grapevine leads that the opposition is listening to is irrelevant from your perspective. What matters is that you have to assume that someone is feeding your competitors within your company information about the skeletons you have in your closets.

Your job is simply to determine the identities of the moles. To do this, pass a deliberate red herring on to one of your primary suspects, then see where this red herring surfaces. If your political enemy acts on the red herring you will have found your leak—and hopefully at the same time caused your enemy to waste time and resources tracking down something that was totally false.

What to do with moles? While termination is usually first on your mind, hold back. These people will be invaluable to you in the long term. They are a means of leaking information to your opposition—a way to trick, mislead, and misdirect your political enemies. The key is to feed them enough accurate information (usually worthless politically) to maintain them as credible sources in the eyes of your enemy. Only feed them additional red herrings or misinformation when it is to your advantage to do so.

5

> War is not merely a political act but a real political instrument, a continuation of political intercourse, a carrying out of the same by other means.
>
> **Karl von Clausewitz**

THE ART OF WAR— CUBICLE STYLE

Make no mistake about it, when it comes to office politics, you are fighting a war, albeit a far-from-conventional one. There's a lot at stake, not just your job but your ability to provide for your family. As with war, there are victories and defeats. And oftentimes the winning of a battle does not mean the winning of the overall war. As with any war, it is planning and coordination that ensure victory. You may not like it but you can't deny it; war and politics are concepts that are one and the same, and as such a study of strategies (and their supporting tactics) is necessary.

What separates the deranged postal worker—the one toting an Uzi into the office to deal with its backstabbing politics— from the intelligent cubicle warrior is the subtlety of strategy. The postal worker has not looked far down the road, whereas

ooks of the Cubicle Warrior Every cubicle warrior should have a number of books ready at hand. The following is a suggested library list of books that you should display proudly on your shelves to let others know that you are not one of the mindless slugs but are willing to draw blood if necessary.

- *Sun Tzu's Art of War.* Translated numerous times, this tome has a great deal of political insight. Don't think of it as a military book, but rather as a book dealing with political survival and strategy.
- *The Prince.* This is Niccolò Machiavelli's study of the art of leadership and survival in Renaissance Italy, where a host of small city-states jockeyed for position. You'll have to do some sifting as you read the material, but there are tidbits that hold true forever.
- *Macbeth.* William Shakespeare's timeless play about a loving couple's bloody rise to political power by killing their rightful king.

the cubicle warrior understands that actions in the present will have a real impact on power and position in the future.

Office politics is war, but it is a different kind of warfare. It is a warfare where bullets are replaced by memos, where bombardments are not by artillery or airpower but by e-mail and fax messages. Generals have titles such as "assistant director," and oftentimes the pivotal individual who turns the tide of battle is not some officer (manager) but Mike from the mail room or Steve from Accounting. Some wars (political and otherwise)

- *War As I Knew It.* These are the memoirs of George S. Patton, one of the greatest generals since Stonewall Jackson. The treatise in the appendix at the end of the book regarding the orders to his army on how to wage war has a wide range of cubicle warfare implications and applications.
- *Animal Farm.* Orwell's look at politics has some interesting insights into coups and rebellion.
- *Silent Coup.* This book by Len Colodny and Robert Gettlin describes the overthrow of President Richard Nixon from office and details what can happen in any office, even the oval one, when people get a taste of power and stretch themselves too thin.
- *Will.* Make no mistake about it, G. Gordon Liddy's book is an insider's look at the ultimate games of office politics and an individual who was in the middle of them all.

are short, others can last decades and cost hundreds of lives or careers, simply to sate someone's ego or personality.

This chapter is designed to assist you in establishing your own strategic direction. If you are going to take an active role in office politics, you will find that determining your strategy helps you determine which tactics are most appropriate. (Tactics are covered in detail in Chapter 6.) If you have no desire to wage politics in your office but simply hope to increase your chances of surviving the battles raging around you, this chapter is also useful—the strategy of simple survival is an essential one that others often overlook and can mean that, when the smoke clears, your career is still intact.

STRATEGIES VERSUS TACTICS

It is important to differentiate what is a strategy from what is a tactic in terms of politics. Strategies consist of several different elements, including:

- Goals and objectives
- A large-scale plan to meet those goals
- How you conduct yourself in meeting those goals (also known as the Rules of Engagement)

First and foremost, a strategy is a long-range objective or goal—what you are working toward. It defines how you can discern when you are successful. For example, in the Gulf War this element of the strategy was defined as the liberation of Kuwait. Strategy is also your overall plan of operations. In other words, again reflecting on the Gulf War, the strategy could be defined in broad terms as using superior air power to blast Iraq into a smoldering heap and then crush whatever military force was left (if anyone) with a vastly superior ground force. Strategy is also your demeanor and conduct in your actions.

Tactics, on the other hand, are the actions undertaken to achieve strategies. In terms of politics and war, tactics are smaller in scope and scale but equally necessary. Again returning to the Gulf War, the tactics called for the suppression of the Iraqi forces, especially their armored fighting vehicles. Tactical strikes were called out against any and all armored vehicles to neutralize them (Read: "blow them up") so they could not be used against the allied ground forces.

In essence, tactics win battles; strategy wins wars. So how does this apply to the sinister world of office politics? Simply put, a professional establishes a strategy for political dealings, then picks the tactics that best implement that strategy.

THE ROLE OF STRATEGY

There are numerous strategies you can use to position yourself in the political arena. How you pick one tells a great deal about you as a person both on an interpersonal level and how you are perceived by the company or organization that you work for.

Working off of the three elements that define what a strategy is, you must first determine the goal or objective that you wish to work toward. Second, you must determine, at least on a macro scale, how you are going to meet that goal. Third—yet of equal importance—you must decide what standards of conduct you are willing to follow as you work toward that goal.

Strategic Goals

For goals to be of any use they must meet two criteria. They must be measurable and achievable. Measurement is typically done over a period of time. (How long will it take for me to ruin Rob's career in Purchasing?) Another example might be more tangible in nature, such as "become vice president of research and development in the next three years."

Achievability is a matter of judgment. Can goals be set too high? Not necessarily. High goals are fine as long as some

hat If I Don't Want to Define a Strategy? Is a strategy necessary? The answer to this is no—but that response comes with some large-scale provisos that should be examined. If you do not establish a political strategy, you are *not* laying down any long-range goals for your career in terms of the power you wish to achieve or hold. Even individuals who do not undertake an active political role in their offices or companies generally have some sort of long-range career goals to work toward.

Such strategy setting is not a requirement but makes prudent sense. If you do not take part in politics and have no career goals, chances are you do not seek anything beyond the desk where you currently sit. You are content with your job and career, your manager, and your income. Of course, you most likely also believe in

realism exists in terms of how long it may take to reach those goals. The phrasing of this is important, since realism implies that you are being realistic. When setting any goal, you must take a serious look at yourself. Not everyone, including you, may have what it takes to be CEO—no matter how badly you think you deserve or want it.

Political and career goals are hopelessly entwined with power in a company. Earlier we discussed how power is measured, and in setting goals the rubber meets the proverbial road. When it comes to establishing your goals there are two aspects that you must consider. One is your personal goals, the other is your professional goals and objectives.

On a personal level, goals usually involve lifestyle, comfort, location, or security (wealth). Personal goals are important to

the Tooth Fairy, Santa Claus, and that Hillary Clinton spends her afternoons baking cookies and vacuuming the Oval Office.

If you are taking on the role of a political player, waging political acts in your company or firm without having a strategy, there is a word that describes you: *sociopathic.* While Career Politicians (see Chapter 7 for details) enjoy playing politics for the sake of playing politics, most of them have some sort of strategy. Destroying careers and ruining projects with no strategy in place, all just for the sake of doing it, is not the mark of a totally sane person but rather an individual weak of character and a potential candidate for membership in Charles Manson's Family or a Son of Sam stand-in.

have, because they often affect how you live and why you are working in the first place. Make no mistake though, these are things that are earned by your political actions (or nonactions) at the office.

Thus the office or professional goals are what drive and motivate your actions during the waking hours. And these professional or work-related goals are the most overriding in terms of importance.

These goals are nominally classified as either power or prestige based. The power-based objectives are those that are centered on the control, maintenance, and wielding of power in your office or organization. Prestige-based goals are those that deal not so much with power but the trappings that are associated with it.

Title Power (Power Goal)   Title power is also known as paper power. It is defined by a position on an organization chart and the authority (and sometimes even responsibility) associated with it. This is similar to the prestige goal of assuming a title, but in this case you covet not the title itself but what the title provides you. For example, setting a goal to become a vice president or a partner (or whatever) is a Title Power goal when it is because of the fact that you will have control over a larger staff, management of a massive budget, and the capability to hire and fire as you desire. Clearly this is not setting a goal for a title, but for what the title can provide.

Tangible or Control Power (Power Goal)   Tangible power is not so much a position on paper but the actual ability to execute actions. It may be signing authority (in terms of dollars) or the capability to start new projects, terminate projects, reorganize operations, and so on. Tangible power can also be mere control over a particular operation or activity.

Usually tangible power is not defined in an employee handbook but is a perceived power. Oftentimes it is not officially sanctioned by management but instead is something that one develops over time.

Control comes into play because oftentimes the real power in an organization centers around who controls certain aspects of that company or firm. For example, the individual who has control over the e-mail system has incredible power since slowing it down (or "inadvertently" cutting it off totally) can shut down most companies. While on paper such an individual does not seem to have much power and may be a middle-level manager, the sheer power that someone in such a position holds can be staggering.

Headcount (Power Goal) Power is often defined in an organization by the number of people reporting to a manager. Oftentimes organizational charts are misleading in regard to this type of power. With the thrust in the 1980s and 1990s to flatten organizational structures, reducing the number of levels, it is possible for low-level managers to have authority over large numbers of people. Likewise, in some companies it is possible for a high-level manager to have few direct reports.

Headcount power goals are driven primarily by maintaining the *need* to hire more people, but growth is threatened by outsourcing or corporate downsizing. Creating that need, the constant requirement of growth, is usually the mainstay of individuals bent on headcount power.

Survival (Power Goal) There are people who simply do not want to take part in politics or, because of their years and current position, simply wish to maintain where they are in terms of position and power. These individuals have a goal of survival.

Individuals seeking survival are not entirely easy to deal with since the goal is one that is based on instinct as well as planning. This goal does not require nearly as much planning as it requires anticipating and reacting to the political environment. Individuals with this as their goal concentrate on not getting ahead but on keeping what they have intact.

Position or Title (Prestige Goal) One of the most traditional goals that individuals aim for is that of position or title; that is, they covet and work toward a job within the organization where they work. They do not seek the power associated with the job; they simply want the title associated with it. An example of this is the person striving to be a vice president because it will look good on the old résumé for the next career move.

Geographic Location or Territory (Prestige Goal)   With large corporations and companies spread out all over the globe, oftentimes an individual's strategic goal is to assume re-location to a particular position or control over a region or ter-ritory. There are many reasons for this. In some companies an assignment overseas (be it a year-long relocation or even serv-ing on an overseas committee) is necessary for long-term sur-vival in that company. Such geographic assignments are often considered part of a manager's career and thus are necessary.

In most circumstance changes in geographic location or as-sumption of duties elsewhere are more personally motivated. For example, having worked 10 years in Detroit, the lure of moving south—almost anyplace south—may have a great deal of appeal for a manager (especially during the winter months). Or this may be a goal of getting an assignment in a geographic location because of its proximity to the main or corporate of-fice, the thought being that the closer you are to the action the better your chances for getting recognized. Usually these kinds of strategic goals do not come into play until later in an indi-vidual's political career, but they are becoming more common as employees and managers begin to view their organizations beyond the confines of their current office or building.

How Will You Meet Those Goals?

> Pick battles big enough to matter, small enough to win.
>
> **Jonathan Kozol**

Setting a goal is important, but determining how you will achieve it is equally as important. A number of aspects come into play when determining how you will achieve the goals that you set out.

Obstacles   First and foremost of these is for you to find out what obstacles, if any, stand between you and your goal. Sometimes these factors make a short list, sometimes just naming them can be a formidable task—depending on how far-reaching your goal is. Analysis (never in writing!) of these elements is crucial to you being able to achieve your goal. The number of potential factors is a long list, varying for each company or firm that you work for. Identifying them can be as simple as asking yourself, Who is now in the position that I desire?

In other words:

- Who is in that position now? How long have they been there? What politics did they use to assume that position? Who does that position report to? What appeals to that manager?
- Does anyone hold the power that I covet, and if so, who?
- What other departments or divisions (groups or teams or pick your buzz word) might be opposed to my assuming the power I desire? How might they react when I make my move? How can I counter that?
- How can I obtain that position or power?
- Is there a job that I have to hold before I step into the final slot that I am aiming for?
- Who else in the organization might be trying to obtain the same strategic goal that I am?
- Is there any corporate trend that might affect my goal—for example, are we downsizing and what will that do?
- Will technology have any impact on the goal that I am setting? If so, how can I exploit it to my advantage?

This is more of an analysis of the barriers that exist or might exist as you strive for your goal. And since change is constant in the universe, you must constantly be reevaluating your goals and the things that may be influencing them.

Tactics   Once you have your hands wrapped around your obstacles, you should select the tactics you plan to counter them. Chapter 6 covers political tactics in more detail, but it is important to know that the list is long and varied. Tactics are the tools of the trade, your weapons of war. As you apply them you will find that some are suited to your personality, taste, and degree of bloodthirstiness. Look them over and select the tactics that best fit your needs and, most important, help you achieve your overall strategic goal.

There are nonpolitical tactics that can come into play as you sculpt your career as well. For example, if it is a company norm that everyone at the vice president level have an MBA or equivalent, then you will have to factor that into your strategic plan. Everything from accepted dress and behavior may or will factor into the nonpolitical goals that you must take into account when putting together your plan.

Your Conduct in the Eyes of Others— The Rule of Impression

"Rules? Rules! We don't need no stinking rules! This is war." There are damn few rules in the world of office politics. Rules in the political arena are more of a matter of how you wish to be perceived politically and how you will project that desired image. In other words, how you conduct yourself in the eyes of your peers versus those you have trampled in your climb to the top.

The Rule of Impression is that your actions create a perception in others as to your political willingness. The key clearly is to manipulate your image in the eyes of others. The best cubicle warriors are either those who are public and open about it, or those whom no one expects to use politics to get ahead. Key to the Rule of Impression is the fact that the way others see you determines how they will interact with you and how likely they are to employ political acts against you. Perception, in this case, often is not reality. Thus when thinking about these perceptions, consider them to be rough guidelines in interacting with others.

There are three things that you can be perceived as, and this will vary depending on who sees you (be it your victims or those who are riding your coattails to the top!). All depend on how you wield politics to achieve your goals.

For example, if you are a person who does not cover your tracks, bury your bodies, or otherwise conceal the truth, you will be seen as a *political player*. In this role, individuals will not trust you, and at the same time they will have a certain amount of fear when you undertake a project. You have used your political power blatantly, and people's code of conduct when dealing with you will be to do the same to you—if possible, strike before you can. Oftentimes your victims will see you as a political player simply because they've seen you in action.

Another common misconception or political perception is that you are *necessarily political*. That is, you only take part in politics when you have to but generally your motivations are for the good of the company or firm. Others have seen you use politics, but only in public when your own career was at stake. They do not fear you using politics and respect the fact that you will stoop to using it when you have to. Their conduct with you generally is more open, which is something that you can later exploit to your own advantage.

Finally, others may see you as *nonpolitical*. Of all the perceptions, this is the most useful if you practice politics or the most dangerous if you are attempting to simply survive in your current company's political storms. If you are active in politics but others believe you are not active, they will not see you for the threat that you really are. They misjudge your skills the greatest with this perception. If they wage political war on you, they suddenly will find themselves dealing with an awakened giant.

If you are not a political player at all, this perception essentially is the same as strapping a neon sign to your side flashing the word *sheep* in front of a pack of hungry wolves. You'll be lucky if they leave a scrap of meat on your bones when they are done. They will strike, manipulate, contort, corrupt, and twist your life, and you will have little if nothing to defend yourself with. Think meat grinder. It is much better, and safer, for them to perceive you as someone who is necessarily political rather than nonpolitical.

COMMUNICATIONS: THE ART OF THE SPIN

> I usually get my stuff from people who promised
> somebody else that they would keep it a secret.
>
> **Walter Winchell**

> He who trusts secrets to a servant makes him his master.
>
> **John Dryden**

As I noted earlier, every office has an informal and yet stunningly effective communications method that defies even the advances of technology . . . the office grapevine. Plainly put, this is where information is passed from person to person. In the office, with the speed that e-mail and voice mail allows, it is possible for a well-placed rumor to reach light speed in a matter of minutes, spreading from person to person like a social disease.

The grapevine is one of the most powerful assets that a cubicle warrior can use, for several reasons. First off, it often has access to information that is not commonly or publicly available to employees. The reason for this is simple: some of the members of these communications networks have access, by nature of their jobs, to information that should remain classified. For example, the secretary typing up the secret list of the next wave of layoffs has considerable clout with the grapevine. In terms of information gathering, the corporate grapevine is often more effective than any individual, ah, intelligence-gathering effort because it can piece together corroborating evidence from several sources and arrive at its own conclusions.

Second, the grapevine often moves faster than normal communications modes. For example, a memo regarding promotions may take a day or two—or several—to work its way through the interoffice mail system. The information contained in the memo, however, can circulate through the same office in the form of verbal or telephone gossip and covert e-mail messages in a matter of hours or even minutes.

From an office politics standpoint, the use of the office grapevine is important. It is a way for you to gather information. Another aspect that is crucial is that access to the grapevine allows you a way to extend your own communications to the company or firm that you work for. In other words, it is a chance for you to put forth your desired image and perspective on company-related issues or personnel—to put your spin on things that affect your political strategy and tactics.

Tapping the Grapevine

There is an old saying in political circles that you do not seek out the company grapevine, it seeks you out. There is an infinite number of ways to tap or access the grapevine in your organization. The key is not how you do it, but with whom you do it.

Finding someone who has access to the grapevine is simple. In any given company or firm, upwards of 80 percent to 90 percent of the employees are receivers of information from this informal communications network. In other words, if you want to hear a rumor, you can ask almost anyone.

Some individuals are more likely to have accurate information than others. Placing information (whether it's accurate or not is irrelevant for the purposes of this book) on the grapevine can be done by finding individuals who are not just receivers but transmitters of gossip. These are people who because of the very nature of their jobs—handling information from all over the company or firm—serve as a means of initiating grapevine information.

The following are some of the best candidates for getting information spread:

- *Secretaries/Administrative Assistants.* They type the memos, set the meetings, and basically can control the people they report to.
- *Mail Room Staff.* Paper still controls most offices—and the mail room staff, despite what most people think, *do* often take the time to read memos. Also they have access to many departments, talk to a lot of people, and generally would rather talk than do their jobs.
- *Copy Room Staff.* Any major meetings or training sessions require a lot of paper—and the Copy Room usually handles it.

- *Administrative Personnel.* While in most offices the old typing pool is a thing of the past, there is still a vast army of administrative personnel running modern corporations or firms. Ignore the traditional org chart; these people hold the tangible power and control the executives and managers they work for—in most cases.
- *Other Managers.* If you want the information with another person's spin, let someone else do the research for you. If you want to launch your own communications or gossip, locate another politically active manager and drop a word to the wise.

Other Communications: That Old Pen and Sword Thing

The grapevine is not the only form of communication that a corporate politician can make use of. There are still the normal forms of written and oral communications that are expected in any organization. This includes e-mail, memorandums, status reports, and so on. What makes these different is the way they're used—a full-fledged office politician uses them to further personal political plans while at the same time inflicting damage on the competition.

This section of *Cubicle Warfare* deals with how to maximize these forms of communications to your advantage.

On Paper or in the Air?   What gets put in writing? Anyone who has been in any office for a significant period of time knows that you only put a few things in writing. First you put things down that are aimed at covering your own butt. To be plain, you document agreements and status items with others so that when something does go wrong, you can hold up the document as some degree of innocence or, if nothing else, plausible deniability.

Another time when written documentation is important is when it is to be used against others. Oddly enough, people are willing to say things to you that they won't put in writing. When that is the case you can document it not just for your own protection, but to hold their proverbial feet to the fire. A common method of doing this is the line added to a commitment-related memo or e-mail that roughly states, "if you do not respond to this in the next X days, I will assume that you concur with the findings stated above." This is the kind of commitment-level communication that cannot be ignored and forces the recipient to respond in some fashion.

If you are involved with office politics, almost everything else in an office should *not* be communicated in writing. The reason is simple—if it's in writing it can be used against you in the future. The age-old marketing phrase has deep meaning in politics: "With air you've got nothing." Thus verbal communications leave people holding nothing that can be verified, confirmed, or authenticated.

If you are reading this tome in hopes of dodging politics in your office, the opposite rule comes into place. In other words, document everything. Documentation is the bane of office politicos—if you can establish yourself early on as the kind of person who documents everything, you tend not to be dragged into as much politics simply out of fear that you might document something that can be used *against* the office politicians.

The Cubicle Warrior's Writing Style In those things that you do put in writing, take full advantage of the medium to execute your political tactics. Writing skills are vital in the contemporary office, since so many employees in today's companies simply cannot write. The most determined office politicians learn this lesson quickly and often are the first to sharpen their writing skills.

What is the difference between the writing of a nonpolitician and a political player? A nonpolitician will state facts in generality. In a status report or memo specific names are avoided, commitments are made only in vague terms. Nonpoliticians try to write nothing that can be held against them lest they get sucked into a political brawl.

At the other extreme, an office politician does not use the pen as if it were a sword but rather as an air-driven chaingun that could mow down a tank as well as a few political opponents. Names are named. Times are quoted. Individuals are framed (if necessary for the greater good). Entire departments are mentioned and their real or perceived levels of participation in the corporate culture dragged through the mud. And to add insult to injury, the politician controls and manipulates who sees the information.

On pages 116 and 117 are two examples of the same memo. The first sample is written by a nonpolitician and is a typical status report for a meeting. The second was written by a political player who is using this simple status report to advance his or her career.

The numbers on this list correspond to the footnote numbers in the second memo:

1. The use of the person's title in the To: field subliminally is a symbol of respect, whether the respect is real or not.
2. The addition of the writer's department indicates that he is speaking for the entire department. Informally the

A typical example of a nonpolitical communication:

IMMA, WEENIE, AND HOSER
Management Consulting Excellence Since 1995

To: Richard Imma
From: Monty Markham
Subject: Minutes of Companywide Reorganization Committee

The following is a summary of the weekly meeting:

- Discussion was given regarding the consultant's proposed changes with the Graphics Division. Members of the committee disagreed as to the best approach to implementing the changes, or if all of the changes were necessary. It was agreed to table discussion of the item until more research could be done by the Publishing Department.
- The Consulting Division feels that there are several human resource issues that need to be addressed before they implement their aspects of the current reorganization plan.
- With the pending layoffs, the Human Resource Department has issued several stern warnings to the department heads on how they communicate layoffs to their staff. Prudent action on all parts is called for to avoid potential legal action.
- Concern was raised by members of the Accounting Department that staffing cuts may impact our managerial accounting reports and shareholder releases.
- The potential for cost savings by reduction of employee benefits was also pesented in lieu of layoffs. Several of the committee members are reviewing this information and its potential impact on their staff's morale before firm action can be made.
- Should you have any further questions, feel free to call me at x5555. Thank you for your interest and support of this activity.

cc: Accounting Department Manager
      Marketing Department Manager
      Consulting Department Manager

A typical example of the same memo, written with full political impact:

IMMA, WEENIE, AND HOSER
Management Consulting Excellence Since 1995

To: Richard Imma, Partner[1]
From: Monty Markham, Technology Department Representative[2]
Subject: Minutes of CRC[3]

The following is a summary of the weekly meeting:

- The Graphics Division is resisting the recommendations of the rest of the committee in regard to cutbacks.[4]
- The Consulting Division has several personnel issues that may result in costly lawsuits in relation to how they are handling the upcoming reorganization. At present they have no plan in place for dealing with these risks.[5]
- The Human Resource Department has issued several stern warnings to the department heads on how they communicate layoffs to their staff. This is most costly to the Consulting and Marketing Divisions where our greatest risks exist.[6]
- The Accounting Department indicated that staffing cuts will impact our managerial accounting reports and shareholder releases. Since this could impact our SEC filings, some sort of investigation may be merited as to why this information was withheld so long.[7]
- The Finance Department recommended cutting back marketing sales incentives as well as executive perks such as the executive management annual retreat. While several members of the committee, led by the Technology Department, opposed this move, others such as Accounting supported it. We have tabled the matter until the next meeting.[8]

Should you have any further questions, feel free to call me at x5555. Thank you for your interest and support of this activity.

cc: Technology Department Manager[9]

---

writer is assuming or declaring he has more power than he may actually hold.

3. The use of an acronym—CRC—for Companywide Reorganization Committee indicates that the person writing the memo understands that in the modern company the acronym is often developed long before its meaning is understood.

4. No pussyfooting around here. Names are given and the Graphics Department looks like it's simply not a team player.

5. The mention of lawsuits and a lack of plans will get upper management's attention and smears the Consulting Division as easily as planting a bloody glove in the director's backyard.

6. A beautiful double slam, sinking more lead into the Consulting group and linking them in the same breath to the Marking Division.

7. This is a use of implication in writing. It is implied that Accounting is withholding information, though not expressly stated. This is likely to attract the attention of upper management to begin wondering what else the department may be hiding.

8. In the original message, the impact was veiled and hidden. In this political draft however, the Technology Department (which the writer is part of) was against cutting back benefits that the recipient of the memo currently enjoys. This is a form of brownnosing (a tactic described in more detail in Chapter 6).

9. Note the differences in the carbon copy list. Here some people, especially those slammed, do not get copies of the memo. The writer has instead attempted to curry favor with his own department's management.

E-Mail Tools at Your Disposal

Every electronic mail system in place has features and functionality that can be used to your advantage either offensively or defensively in terms of political goals and tactics. While this varies from software package to software package, there are some commonalties that exist that everyone in an office should learn and use where appropriate.

The following is the short list of these features:

- *Return Receipt.* This allows you to receive automatic confirmation back via e-mail when someone has opened the e-mail you've sent. This does not mean that your target has actually read it or understood it, simply that he or she has opened it. This is used best when dealing with individuals given to lying about communications, that is, "I never got that message." Nothing is more joyous than to reply, "Then who was reading your e-mail on Wednesday at 10:04 A.M.?"

  There are variations to this feature in some mail systems that allow you to receive confirmation when someone receives the mail *and* when they open it to read. Both of these have similar political implications.

- *Saving a Copy of Your Messages.* While costly in terms of disk space (fortunately, prices are cheap for larger hard drives), this allows you to retain a copy of what you've sent. This is useful for confirming that you've performed tasks or that the proper communications were indeed sent out. Furthermore, you can pull up this already-sent mail and resend it to others should the need exist.

- *Blind Carbon Copy.* This feature in some mail systems allows you to send copies to individuals without their names appearing on the CC list. In other words, no one but you and the blind-copy recipient know about the copy. This is an excellent way to covertly send e-mail messages to other management levels without incurring the direct wrath of your own manager.

- *No Copying.* Several e-mail software packages have a feature that will prevent an individual receiving a mail message that you sent from forwarding it or copying it to a word processor or other software package. This allows you a high degree of control as to who sees the information and forces the recipient to pass it on either via the grapevine or by hard copy.

TELESTABBING: TELECOMMUTING, HOTELING, AND BACKSTABBING

The trend toward people working at home (telecommuting) has as yet had little impact on the world of office politics, but there are some implications that need to be taken into account. The telecommuter works wherever the notebook computer is currently plugged in. Many companies are starting to use what they call *hoteling*—where the individual does not even maintain a physical office with the company, but instead checks in whenever necessary to make use of the facilities that the company or firm has to offer.

What does this do to office politics? One thing is that the maxim "out of sight, out of mind" does not apply in this case. Telecommuters use e-mail, voice mail, and the telephone so much that people often feel as if they *are* actually in the same office building rather than working at home. Face-to-face confrontations are more limited, but the extensive use of other communications forms makes these people just as viable in the political arena.

At the same time, if you disdain politics, then telecommuting is not exile to Siberia but parole to Aruba. Working out of your house, you are physically isolated from politics and oftentimes people do not target you in their games or tactical actions—you are nowhere near them and don't look like a viable threat or wedge against others. If you hate politics, begin telecommuting.

What is different for the telecommuter who is savvy to the ways of politics? Some of the traditional icons of power do not appeal to the telecommuter as they do to someone in the office. Having the bigger office or the key to the executive garage simply isn't important if you don't work in the office. These are factors that everyone will have to take into account in their dealings with this growing army of corporate wage slaves.

6

Power corrupts. Absolute power is kind of neat.

John Lehman

TACTICS

This chapter deals with the tactics of waging cubicle warfare. For most people who live and breathe in business, this is where they will see (and experience) politics firsthand. At the tactical level, battles are fought and won. Strategic politics can take months or years to execute, but tactics happen often daily or even hourly.

Each of the tactics covered in this chapter is detailed so that you can spot the most common uses and applications, or so you know how it is used. The Impact section covers something of the scope of the tactics, or the most common results of using such tactics successfully. Some tactics ruin careers or provide advancement, others merely erode those whom they are used against.

Most important is the Countermeasures section. For each tactic, this section provides you with ways to either defeat it or to at least minimize the damage. If you're reading for self-defense, this is an important section because it will help you survive the day-to-day fights that rage either openly or covertly in your office.

CHOOSING APPROPRIATE TACTICS

A lot of tactics are available to the cubicle warrior. Some of them are age-old, while others are relatively new thanks to influxes of technology and office trends. So how do you determine which tactics to use?

That depends. What are your morals? Just how low are you willing to go? Make no mistake, some of the ploys outlined in this chapter can cost people their jobs given the right circumstances. If you seek to use this book to wage political warfare, you must weigh carefully what tactics to use based on your own management style and what results or risks you are willing to live with.

There is more than guilt and morality to factor in when picking your tactics. What tactics best suit your corporate culture? Will your management respond negatively to a particular tactic, or will their style actually work to your advantage? These are not factors that can be laid out on paper, so rely on your own gut feelings and readings of your company's or firm's culture and how its management reacts. Much of this can be determined through good intelligence, but common sense and logic play a role and no book can walk you through how to think.

Finally, you must evaluate how the intended target of these tactics will respond to them. Nothing is static in the office. Don't ever assume that political opponents or targets of your tactical advances will simply sit back idly and allow you to stab them in the back. They will resist, attempt to counterattack in some cases, and even launch their own political offensive if given the opportunity. You have to plan on this, anticipate their reaction, and plan a counter to it.

APPLYING TACTICS
AND COUNTERTACTICS

Victory goes to the player who makes the next-to-last mistake.

Chess Master Savielly Grigorievitch Tartakower

Key phrase here: Don't be stupid. *Cubicle Warfare* is designed to walk you through a particular tactic (and its countertactics) step-by-step and offer you variants and different approaches. In the real world nothing is that cut and dried. The tactics listed here are not always going to work (as ought to be obvious).

Why not? First off, the viability of a tactic or its countermeasure is often driven by your company's culture and history in terms of office politics. In other words, some things will work in your environment, others will not. What you have to do is apply something lacking in many offices: common sense. Take a serious look at what you are intending to do, and if it seems logical and if your instincts tell you that it is an appropriate tactic, it may be workable.

Timing is another factor that cannot be defined but can often determine the success or failure of a tactic or defensive move. When launching a political assault you should plan on initiating the tactic when it will have the maximum impact. Likewise when you are fending off an attack by someone, how you time your defensive countermeasure could determine its overall impact.

There are three guidelines in regard to timing that should be examined:

- Strike when least expected.
- Initiate your attack or defense when your opponent has the least time or resources to respond.
- Attack with enough force to win. Nothing is gained in initiating a tactic that has no hope of success.

The concept of hitting when your foe least expects it takes keen awareness of your foe and good intelligence gathering. In laymen's phrasing, it is hitting your enemies when they are down. Seems unfair? Wrong. Remember, your political foes will do the same thing to you. If you are seeking to survive your corporate culture, when you are at your lowest is when you should be most prepared to fend off another assault.

The second principle of timing, hitting when your foe cannot muster resources or when there isn't enough time to properly counterattack, is also appropriate. This is not a matter of honor, but one of corporate survival. Some of the best political assaults (or defenses) are launched on Friday afternoons when people are leaving the office and unable to rally their troops or put their spin on the necessary communications. Likewise hitting on, during, or near holidays or people's vacations is also appropriate if you seek to maximize your impact.

THE TACTICS OF THE BATTLE

This section lists the tactics of office politics. Read on at your own risk.

Brownnosing for Fun and Profit

Brownnosing, by definition, is attempting to curry favor from management based not on job performance but on interpersonal favoritism. Often in its illustrious and successful existence it has gone by other names—kissing up, buttering up, bootlicking, butt kissing, ass kissing, butt wiping—brownnosing is something that has reached a nearly art-form status with many managers.

Brownnosing works. Most companies or firms don't admit it, they may even refuse to acknowledge its existence, but it is effective. Why? Simply put, brownnosing appeals to the egos of the targets. As humans, our egos often govern our decision-making ability. We also tend to surround ourselves with those who think and act like us as managers. Brownnosers, by their actions, show that they either like us or support us. Either way it appeals to the egos of the targets and fulfills that need to have others working for us who like us.

In its mildest form, brownnosing is simply complimenting your management food chain in an effort to gain their support or at least get them to acknowledge you. It can take a personal form, for example, "Gee, Ms. Watson, you're looking great today." This form of brownnosing is often referred to as "Pulling an Eddie" or "Haskilling," taking its name from the prototype of bootlickers, Eddie Haskill of *Leave it to Beaver* fame.

Brownnosing most often takes form in work-related compliments. For example, "Sir, I just don't understand why the management committee doesn't listen to your proposal on the matter. . . ." or "I'm just thankful I don't have your job and have to deal with hassles at your level, sir." These statements do not

he Ultimate Countermeasure: Work! Politics is something that requires time to take part in. One of the most common ways of countering internal politics is a relatively simple one—keeping up a high workload on employees.

The logic here is simple: If people are too busy working they won't have time for playing political games. And to a certain extent, this is sound logic . . . if you view things only in the short term. In the here-and-now, swamping employees with work can drain energy and momentum from almost every kind of office political tactic that is in motion.

deal with personal traits, but instead are related to topics centric to the organization where you work.

Whatever form of brownnosing you choose is based on the managers or individuals you are talking to. Depending on their personalities, you should apply whichever form is most appropriate. Observe your target, get to know what works best there. Does he seem to spend thousands on new suits? This might be an indication that he is a target for a potential Haskilling. Does she work excessive hours and seem to have her entire life preempted by work? Then it may be more prudent to concentrate on work-related brownnosing efforts.

The long-term effectiveness of brownnosing is limited since it is based on its application to a specific manager. Managers often change and when they do, the brownnoser has to seek out a new scent. Also, in a true crisis, management may not rely on the brownnoser. While brownnosing is a good tactic for short-term advances, if the situation is one of panic or crisis, management support for someone who is a bootlicker rather than a good scapegoat or doer is limited.

In the long term however, this can backfire. If you keep a high workload flowing to the rank and file, they will begin to think of the office as a sweatshop. And, worse yet, they will find others in the office to commiserate with about being buried in mounds of paperwork and blurry-eyed from staring at their monitors.

Eventually politics will creep in. Slowly at first, but the exhausted staff will actually bond together (even on their own personal time) to initiate political tactics aimed at slowing down the workload or pace.

Impact   The impact of brownnosing is relatively limited. It helps with securing promotions or assignment to projects, but its long-term impact is limited. It also lacks impact in high-pressure situations and environments.

Countermeasures   How do you defeat or diminish a brown-noser? The best way is to erode a brownnoser with the rest of the work group. Oddly enough, while brownnosing is one of the most widely used tactics in office politics, it is also the one that most people seem to dislike the most. No one likes to see someone get ahead simply because they kissed up to the boss . . . even other brownnosers.

If you see someone getting ahead based on this tactic, let others in the office know about it. Mangle the ass-kisser's reputation. Attach that brownnosing label. Let your grapevine contacts know who's using this tactic. Even if a brownnoser stops and changes tactics, the taint will always stick and people will suspect that any advances—even years down the line—may stem from early bootlicking.

Another viable counter is to establish your own communication with the manager. The impact of a simple line such as "Bob,
I know that Sue got her promotion on merit, but everyone else
in the office feels it's because she's kissing up to you" can go a
long way with managers. While brownnosers hate to be called
out for what they are, it makes a manager feel even worse to be
seen as playing favorites based on ego stroking.

Don't Raise the Bridge, Lower the River

Not everyone in the company or firm that you work for is
a superstar. In fact, most people are far from it. The key in
many organizations is not necessarily to be that superstar but
to *look* like you are, especially when compared to your peers
and counterparts.

How do you do that? Rather than being great yourself, you
lower the perception of everyone else. As you lower the perceived value of your peers, you can oftentimes stand out as
someone who is better. The Lower the River approach is akin
to saying, "I may not be great, but compared to those idiots
around me I'm a god [or goddess]." It is a cousin of brownnosing, but is more aimed at subtle sabotage of management's perceptions of your peers, rather than a blatant attempt to kiss up
to your boss.

Eroding management's belief in everyone else requires very
strong communications skills and equally strong business acumen. They key is to not make this a personal attack. It is a professional attack. You are aiming your sights not at an individual,
though indirectly you hope to take them out. Instead you target
their projects, personnel, departments, and so on.

Your goal is to point out aspects that others are either over-
looking or attempting to bury. When executing the Lower the

River tactic, you must be keenly aware of the weak points in almost every aspect of your peers and fully ready to exploit them. For example, if a manager at your level is way over budget but is pressing to get a new project, you simply point out in the next staff meeting the need for bringing budgets and forecasts under control. The shot is not personal, but it subconsciously flags or reminds your supervisor that there is something amiss, lowering your target's status in the supervisor's eyes.

One vital aspect of this tactic is that it is not a direct assault. You are not pounding on the table saying, "Susan and Marcus are morons!" Instead you are gradually, slowly, and methodically eroding their management support. Wherever they are weak, you are reminding management of the importance of that area. Whenever they are attempting to hide or bury a problem, you make sure that it gets mentioned in front of management. By lowering management's perception of your peers over time, you appear to be better, stronger, more intelligent.

If you opt for this tactic, you should know that you will draw scrutiny from your peers, even if your verbal or written jabs are subtle. You need to have your house in order before you launch this tactic. Make sure that you've not overlooked anything obvious or your peers will be all over you.

Impact   This tactic is really aimed at long-term use. In the short term it is not very effective. Long term, however, it can help pave the corridors of power. Its biggest drawback is that it requires a lot of time, effort, and expertise to maintain over such a long period of time.

Countermeasures   A deft corporate politician will be able to pull off the Lower the River tactic right in front of everyone without becoming open to scrutiny. There are a few easy counters to this, however, all of which depend on the intelligence of your management and your own interpersonal (communications) skills.

The first counter is to use this tactic yourself. What makes the tactic work in the first place is that the user stands taller than the others by lowering their appearance. If you observe people starting to use this tactic, apply it to them as well. Point out their attempts to cover up blunders. Point out their mistakes and oversights just as they are doing with yours. This should be done subtly over time as well, just as the tactic itself is applied against you. Once people realize that they too are being lowered, it can counter their desire to use this tactic.

The other and more popular counter to this tactic is to portray the individual using the Lower the River method against you as a poor team player or as a very negative individual. This is more fun as a counterattack since you can do it directly. For example, "Ross, I appreciate your concern over my budget, but this isn't the point of the meeting and such actions really erode our team's spirit." Management almost always feels uncomfortable supporting someone who is not "on the team" or is negative in the eyes of the rest of the staff since supporting that person can reflect poorly on the manager's own leadership style.

Lies, Lying, and All Parts Between

> Hateful to me as the gates of Hades is that man who
> hides one thing in his heart and speaks another.
>
> **Homer**

No book on office politics would be complete without a discussion of lies. Truth is subject to interpretation in most offices.

Gather enough data and crunch it hard enough and you can justify any point, any argument, almost any position. Since the truth is always questionable, so are lies.

Lying is something that is more common in an office than most people wish to admit, especially an office boiling over with politics and backstabbing. People who seek to use this tactic can be stunningly successful. Lies, until exposed for what they are, are truths to those who hear them. People are willing to believe lies in many cases even when presented with hard facts contradicting the lies. And even when a lie is fully exposed and laid bare on the table, the liar can often still salvage a victory by creating doubt in others with the lie. In doubt, fear and paranoia often flourish.

There are risks with lies however, and oftentimes it is these risks that drive people away from this tactic. The risk in a lie comes from being identified as the liar (the source of the lie) and being confronted with the truth. Thus a successful liar tries to work around these factors so as to avoid facing these risks.

First and foremost, a lie is the kind of thing that should never risk getting traced back to its creator. To do this, the liar must maximize the use of the grapevine or have others release the information in such a way that, even if they are confronted, they will never admit where they got it. This can be done by leaving the information for them to steal and release on their own or giving it to them in confidence, allowing the person who spreads the lie to be faced with guilt if confronted with it. Since most people can only deal with one thing at a time, such a person will not violate a confidence while being confronted as the source of a lie.

And the best way to maintain a lie in the face of the truth is to develop a rival truth. Facts, figures, spreadsheets, formulas, and databases are all designed by bureaucrats to promote their own versions of the truth. When sculpting a lie, a liar needs to assume that at some point the truth will show up. How to justify the lie? Is it possible to fabricate the figures and facts necessary to support the position? Is there someone else who could serve as the source for the information? A liar with some forethought can simply state another version of the facts, rather than turn red-faced and admit to being a liar.

It is also necessary to keep in mind that lies take on a life of their own on the corporate grapevine. From the time someone starts spreading a lie, it will grow, become distorted, and be added to or twisted as it goes. It's always safest for the liar to assume that this will happen from the start.

In terms of the scope or size of the lie, there is no real limit. The concept of the "big lie"—the bigger the lie the more people will believe it—is based in reality, not in fantasy. Corporate culture becomes a ready source of fuel to add to lies. Are layoffs rumored to be due? Are people tense and willing to believe the unbelievable? Liars use this kind of information to their advantage, remembering it is best to use a big lie rather than a small one since the risks are virtually the same.

Truly masterful liars always keep one concept in mind: tell the people what they want to hear. In the corporate environment this can mean that they want to hear how bad certain managers are. They want to hear how screwed up the company or firm is. They like to hear about internal political slugfests or who is sleeping with whom. Liars feed on those kinds of emotions as much as they can.

Impact   Lies have long-range and lasting impact. There are risks associated with lying, however, and they are substantial.

Overuse of this tactic can also erode someone's long-term credibility in an office. A political player cannot survive on lying alone.

The final word on the impact of lies is that they don't die. In fact, once they start, they are impossible to stop.

Countermeasures Lies are difficult to defeat. First of all, even in the face of the blatant truth, people will often believe a lie. This is not to say that you cannot take on a co-worker or peer who is lying, it simply means that you have to do it using the same sort of tools that generated the lie—primarily making use of the company grapevine and taking the time to carefully sculpt your countermessage of truth.

Take a good look at what makes a good lie but apply it to the truth. Make it a message that the people want to hear, such as "Jim was simply playing politics, trying to backstab Jill because she humiliated him in sales in the last quarter." People *want* to hear about infighting, corruption, greed, and power. Make sure your version of the truth has these elements and it is an easy sell to the company grapevine. While it is a covert approach, oftentimes this is the best way of dealing with a lie, especially if the liar is in a position where direct confrontation is difficult if not impossible.

If the individual who created the lie was sloppy, there is always a chance for a direct confrontation. Before you do this, make sure of a few things. One, do you know the true source of the lie? Two, what spin is the liar likely to place on the lie ("Gee, according to the report I got from Johnson, it looked like you were skimming money from the overseas accounts, Frank. . . ."). Three, will your target simply lie again to get out of it?

If you plan to confront a liar you should plan ahead of time for these contingencies as best you can. Make sure that you understand that a truly good liar will do everything possible to avoid being tagged as such.

For a more long-term solution, if your political foes use this tactic too much you can erode their credibility on a grand scale. *"Don't listen to Louis on these matters, everyone knows that he is a liar."* Mentally keep track of lies and liars and, if you believe that the time is ripe, you can cripple someone long term from using this tactic by simply attaching the liar label.

The Bypass

Every organization has some degree of structure—in fact, that's one of the things that helps define what an organization is in the first place. Everyone except the owners or partners or CEO or president reports to someone else. The bypass tactic is aimed at exploiting the hierarchy of such businesses to your personal gain.

A bypass occurs when you establish a personal communications channel to your manager's boss (or even higher). This bypasses your direct manager and gains access to a higher level of management, thus controlling or at least contributing to the information flow that upper management is receiving.

What makes the bypass so appealing is that it allows you to essentially move around someone who may be controlling your career or job. When successfully implemented, a bypass cuts off the targeted manager from information, while at the same time providing the next level up with communications from the individual using this tactic.

Bypasses allow you to circumvent the normal organizational and political structure of your office. They provide you with the means of not dealing with your own management since you are simply working around them rather than with them.

In organizations where there are multiple tiers of management, the bypass is common. Many higher-level managers do not trust those working for them. They believe that information is manipulated, twisted, and filtered to them. *Often with good reason; they did the same thing when they were at that level.* To the eyes of the manager who is on the receiving end of a bypass, this is a chance to get information closer to the root with no filtering or spin put on it. This helps such managers gauge how honest their own direct reports are—making them willing participants in this tactic in many cases.

A side benefit of bypasses is that they are covert enough that most managers are not aware of being the victim of such a tactic. It is also difficult to prove that this tactic is being used against you. Oftentimes upper management will not openly confess to their staff where they got information, unwilling to sever (permanently) the bypassee from his or her communications network.

Executing a bypass is not difficult. It almost always requires some degree of discretion, however—that is, you should not being seen or heard doing it. The corporate myth of an open door policy often paves the way for any employee to establish communications with higher-level management. Oftentimes sitting in for your manager in a meeting (in some companies or firms this is a common practice) gives you the exposure necessary to establish the bypass.

he Open Door Policy Myth   In the 1970s someone began a corporate myth known as the *open door policy.* The concept behind this buzzword is that every manager's door is open to employees should they have concerns or issues that they need to address. The implication to most naive employees is that they can go in under complete anonymity and discuss important business matters with management and the discussion will not be held against them.

This is one of the greatest lies ever put over on cubicle warriors and mindless slugs worldwide. First of all, the open door is often closed—how often have you heard, "Have you discussed this with your manager first?" Second of all, the implied anonymity of the meeting is more in

In executing this tactic, it is necessary to maintain what looks like the moral high ground with the upper-level manager. Think of it in this light: you are not opening this line of communication to undermine your own manager. No, no, no. You are doing this for the best interests of the company. You are concerned that some important information may not be properly passed to upper management—and being a good little corporate soldier, you are simply doing your duty to let management know what is happening "in the trenches."

Impact   The bypass is best used in organizations that are deep in management levels. Flat organizations tend to reduce its effectiveness overall.

In terms of scope of impact, this tactic can be used both short and long term. It is most effective in the long term in efforts to

the imagination of the worker than in reality. All too often, as soon as the employee has walked out, the manager is on the phone with the employee's boss talking about who just came in and what was said.

The problem with this so-called policy is that there is no structure to support it or to punish a manager who has abused it. Thus, other than a chance to rat on the boss to the boss's manager or to establish your own bypass tactic, there is little use or function in this policy other than to convince newly hired staff that the office is a warm, friendly, and safe place to work.

Final word on the "Open Door"—don't let it hit you in the butt as you leave.

---

undermine your own manager or boss. If this is part of your long-term political strategy and your direct manager is the intended target, the bypass can be both effective and efficient.

Countermeasures   Two points of view have to be considered in terms of countermeasures for this tactic. One is as an observer watching a co-worker use this tactic. The other is as the intended victim of a bypass attempt.

If you see a co-worker running a bypass: The best course of action is to inform the targeted manager of the attempt. This may paint you as a snitch or squealer or rat, but will (if the manager has any guts at all) put an end to the effort.

Another viable approach, should you be daring enough to try it, is to set up your own bypass with the same target manager and contradict the information your co-worker is passing.

This has a dual impact. One, it calls the integrity and honesty of the co-worker into question, always useful with a real or potential political target. Two, it can further undermine your own boss, who will appear to the upper manager to have lost control of your unit.

If you are the victim of a bypass effort: You have two basic options. First, take it to the employee. Imply strongly that you know what is going on and what has been said—even if it's not true; nothing shakes somebody up like the feeling of being betrayed in return. Point out that the open door policy works only if your people start with you *before* running to your manager. This is a confrontational, direct, and blunt discussion. Don't go into this kind of meeting being a wet noodle, go in with guns a blazin'.

Second, you can take the matter to your own manager. Undermine the credibility of the employee who attempted the bypass. You may or may not tell your manager that your employee was only trying to spread false information—this aspect isn't that important really and is dependent on your manager to begin with. Don't do this with malice, but be subtle. Strike too hard and your manager might think you are trying to cover up something. If you get too enthusiastic about squashing that little political backstabber who is running to your boss or your boss's boss, you might just inadvertently a give the rat credibility with your management—which is the last thing you want to do.

Point to any ongoing management issues you have with the employee, making sure your own manager understands that you are in charge and handling the personnel situation. The use of the word *personnel* is important. It implies that this is not a personal matter but one involving employee performance.

Indirectly, it implies that the employee trying the bypass is a loose cannon of sorts, running amok in the company or firm.

Death by Committee

> What is a committee? A group of the unwilling,
> picked from the unfit, to do the unnecessary.
>
> **Richard Harkness**

Committees, task forces, focus groups, teams, panels, employee councils, and so on are seen by management as the cogs and gears that turn the massive corporate machine, moving it forward, upward, and onward. In reality, this group of names all refer to gatherings of people who innocently act as leeches, slowly and methodically draining the momentum of a company, bleeding it dry with nonproductive work and effort.

Death by Committee is a common tactic aimed specifically at stalling or slowing an opponent's project, draining company or firm resources, or otherwise grinding a plan or project to a screeching halt. It is an excellent way to make sure that your political opposition cannot move forward, and given its acceptability in most companies, the use of this tactic is considered not only viable, but part of conducting business normally.

Why does a committee maul or cripple a project? Simply put, most teams or committees or groups or task forces do not work productively. While management sees them as a means of bringing the right people into a room to arrive at a common goal, the reality is very different. People come in with a wide range of often-conflicting agendas. They often are not given a common goal to work toward, but rather are there to protect their own political or power interests or territory.

Add to that, most meetings held by this cadre of pointless titles are not effective. Many factors keep committees from getting anything useful done:

- *Nothing to do.* Many meetings lack an obtainable goal set by a single manager. This manager has to be high enough to ensure that everyone participating will adhere to the common goal.

- *No valid deadline.* Meetings often do not have time deadlines set on them, that is, "You must reach a consensus by March 10." Or worse yet, they are given time deadlines that are impossible to achieve.

- *No agenda.* Many corporate meetings lack even a basic agenda. This allows the participants to run amok with no guideline in place as to what gets discussed or worked on.

- *No authority.* Teams or task forces are told to arrive at a decision of some sort, but are not given the authority to make it happen. This is that whole "empowerment" concept-thingy. Thus bazillions of hours are wasted arriving at decisions that management simply ignores or disregards.

- *No key players.* The wrong people are usually named to committees or task forces in the first place.

- *No defense against groupthink.* For those of you unfamiliar with the concept, groupthink is the tendency for meeting participants to go along with the majority even if the majority is dead wrong. *Note: This is often how we elect presidents of the United States as well.* Groupthink provides plausible deniability. No one person makes a bad decision in a committee. Committees maintain innocence and a sense of security because only individuals are fired—never entire committees.

- *No functioning chair.* Good meeting facilitators—people who can lead a meeting effectively—are few and far between in most organizations. And when they do exist, the more politically savvy keep them out of meetings where Death by Committee is being executed.
- *Nobody there.* Far too many meetings are unproductive because weak-kneed managers allow their underlings to blow off meetings. Or worse, some managers encourage this behavior by pulling their staff out of important meetings or assigning them work to ensure they can't attend in the first place.

Given all these factors, it's easy to see the underlying principles that make Death by Committee work as a tactic. Rather than allow something to happen that works to your disadvantage, you can suggest that a committee or task force look into the matter. If one of your political opponents is planning on kicking off a new project or initiative, you can easily suggest that a committee be formed to evaluate the viability of the project.

Once management buys into the idea of forming a committee or task force, you can further derail and bog down the entire process by making sure that the wrong people get invited to participate as members. Successful use of this tactic also allows you to take part in the meeting, bringing up side issues and making sure that the goal (if ever stated or declared by management in the first place) is never achieved.

Impact   Death by Committee is highly effective for a number of reasons. Committees are commonplace in most companies, and it is natural for many managers to form such groups so that they personally are not held accountable for decisions.

The tactic is primarily aimed at slowing or preventing decisions or consensus-building efforts, namely those sponsored by your political opposition. Committees breed other committees, spawn more meetings, and methodically suck energy and momentum from a company. If you want to make sure that something does not get done in a timely manner, assign that task to a committee or task force.

Countermeasures   Beating this tactic requires a great deal of organization and legwork, but it can be accomplished. Meetings have to be managed to defeat Death by Committee. They have to be productive, work off an agenda, and have the right people in place from the start.

If you want to succeed in a company that is plagued with the use of this tactic, you need to develop some strong facilitation skills. This teaches you how to manage and execute an effective meeting.

When you are involved in such meetings, assume a leadership role. Take responsibility for minutes, agendas, invitations, whatever you can to place you in some degree of control of the meeting. Don't worry about stepping on too many toes. It's not like people are clamoring to take minutes or put out agendas—right? Once you have responsibility, it is much easier for you to run the meeting or committee in an organized fashion.

Elements necessary for an effective committee or task force include (but are not limited to):

- A realistic and obtainable goal
- A time deadline that is possible to reach
- Membership on the committee by the people empowered to make the decisions necessary to obtain the goal
- Strict agendas that the members agree to adhere to

■ An individual running the committee who can properly manage and facilitate the meetings that come out of the committee
or task force

Riding the Corporate Craze du Jour

Riding corporate crazes is also known as buzzword management. Every two years or so, someone writes a book (not with
this publisher though—right, guys?) that creates a whole new
management craze. This craze is forged with a good buzzword
that allows for easy marketing of the product, and the corporate world sinks its teeth into the new management trend du
jour as if it were the latest junk food sensation. (*Author's Note:
Just as a point of clarification,* cubicle warfare, *while technically a
buzzword, is not one of these mindless hollow crazes . . . oh no, no,
no. Instead, this is a substantial work of art, a milestone in American literature. Craze, no. Piece of American history—yes.*)

A key element of most of these crazes is that they are written
by consultants to industry. They write these books to make
money and to generate more money through selling consulting
to companies dumb enough to hop on the bandwagon. Which
basically means that the management craze's only substantial
element is the buzzword used by the publisher to sell the material. Content isn't important.

The results of these marketing efforts is that managers buy the
books and trainers and consultants sell training wrapped around
the consultant's buzzword and the theme of the book. And companies or firms out there drop millions hopping on the bandwagon lest their competition start an initiative before they do.
This explains the countless failed Total Quality Management,
Business Process Reengineering, Employee Empowerment, and

Change Management initiatives that have cost the corporate world billions of dollars in lost time, productivity, and manpower.

Office politicians can smell a new buzzword craze a million miles away and use it to their advantage. Using the ploy of "Our competition may be kicking off their own program of this _____ (fill in the blank with the appropriate buzzword name)," corporate politicos will use this kind of program to reorganize the company to their own needs.

Buzzword programs and trends are useful in politics because of the disruption that they cause. Implementing a new corporate culture, restructuring, reorganizing, outsourcing, and all the associated team-building and training exhaust budgets and grind productivity to a halt (ironically the opposite effect that they all claim will be the result of implementing them).

An active cubicle warrior will hop aboard a program of this type for several reasons. It's a prime opportunity to disrupt the programs of opponents within the company or firm—especially if the political opposition's departments become pilot groups for testing out the new programs, something a deft politician can arrange with a bit of maneuvering. The collateral damage of such programs is that they often dishearten the department or group members and tie down critical projects since the personnel are constantly in training, breakout groups, and so on.

All of this is usually done under the guise of "I'm trying something new to make the company better." Refusal on the part of a manager to take part in such programs is often interpreted (Read: "spun by the grapevine") as resistance to change, new ideas, and so on. If planted in the mind of upper management properly, it is nearly impossible for another manager to openly refuse to take part in such programs without risking credibility.

One might argue that even though buzzword programs are not productive on the short term, on the long term they can be very successful. Sometimes, rarely, this is true. However, it is important to understand that companies do not operate on a long-term view. Most only see as far ahead as their next quarter or the upcoming stockholder meeting. Most do not have the foresight and long-range vision to see these programs through to a successful implementation. In the middle of their efforts to kick off such programs, companies tend to cut off the necessary support—especially as management, looking for productivity gains, doesn't see the gains.

Instrumental to the success of this tactic is to be the individual who can guide upper management to undertake these programs—and apply them to your enemies. Placement on committees dealing with company restructuring, process management, and so on is critical. You also have to maintain a watch of the bestseller lists to see what new trend is rocking the country. Finally, you need the ear of upper management to pass on the new trend or buzzword program.

Impact   This tactic is generally not effective against an individual personally, but it's deadly when aimed at departments or work teams. It is also an excellent tactic for slowing or damaging a specific project.

Impact is short-lived at best. People's careers can be damaged by this kind of assault, but generally they are not totally destroyed. This is a move to use if your intent is to slow down a critical project or phase of a project, or if you wish to weaken a political opponent's team.

Countermeasures Buzzword programs must be met on several different levels. If you are a manager who is the target of this trend management approach, your best bet is to point out the impact of this program on your short-term goals and objectives—making sure management is aware of the damage that such programs will have.

You also can take the approach of embracing the program and doing everything you can to make it successful in the shortest period of time. This is the usual approach when your management does not listen to reason and still insists on implementing the measures. It can take a heavy toll on your staff and your group or department or team's productivity, but it is a good way to turn around a bad situation and throw it back at the politico who tossed it into your lap to begin with.

Another viable counterattack is to research a different buzzword program and initiate this tactic back on the one who volunteered your department for implementing such a program. The best defense is often a good offense, such is the case with internal politics.

Stress Manipulation—Going for Stroke

Stress is a byproduct of our society and of the politics in our offices. Some individuals deal with stress well, others do not. Stress affects everyone, employees and managers alike, regardless of how well they seem to cope with it.

Politicos who play real hardball set out to increase the personal level of stress in their opponents to the point where the opponents are unable to function effectively. While this author would never conceive of the use of this tactic to drive a person to a stroke or heart attack, such things often result when someone does not deal well with stress.

There are a wide range of sources of individual mental stress. A political schemer determines who can create stress for a manager. The clients? The next-higher manager or boss? Peers, co-workers, even the secretary? The spouse, parents, and children? And there is the workplace itself—not just the environment but the workloads, deadlines, never-ending nonproductive meetings, and so on. It's a miracle that more people don't buy rifles and climb up on the rooftop to achieve their own form of "venting frustration."

Stress manipulation is a low tactic in terms of the lack of morality involved. It is because of this that you don't see it used too often. But just the same, it is important to know that some individuals, lacking moral fiber, are more than willing to drive you into premature hair loss.

This tactic involves striking at an individual personally, hitting below the belt. In many cases it causes physical pain, ulcers, gas, and so on. It is very dangerous, because some people cannot deal with stress. Anyone attempting this tactic must know when to stop before a co-worker commits suicide, goes postal, or simply drops dead; enough is enough.

How does someone escalate a co-worker's stress levels? There are a number of ways to do this on both a physical level and a mental level. The following list gives you some idea of the wide range of options that you may witness in action. The stress-manipulator will look for opportunities to:

- Take the intended victim out for greasy, high-fat-content lunches.
- Pass the salt, even when it's not asked for. Increasing blood pressure helps maintain a high-stress diet.

aging Psychological War   Also known as a Brain Screw or worse names, this subsidiary tactic is aimed at simply messing with the mind of the person targeted for a full-blown heart seizure.

It's done by altering the target's environment slightly in subtle ways aimed at driving the target insane (or worse). It is best done against an anal-retentive target, but can work on almost anyone.

Some ploys you may see:

- Each day, the office furniture shifts slightly. The perpetrator moves the victim's desk away from the wall a quarter of an inch a day, for example.
- Things on the victim's desk move around. The perpetrator shuffles the position of the in-box, phone, stapler, and so on every night.

- Make sure the coffee is always brewing—full caffeine, of course, with extra cream and triple sugar. People who are wound up like a weasel on speed will never be able to make a sound decision.
- Light that cigarette. Smoking does not lower stress levels— and it's hard to tell whether getting a former smoker to backslide or getting a nonsmoker to start causes more damage.
- Introduce alcohol. Some people deal with stress by taking up other vices such as drinking. Nothing quite like a hangover on the day of a big presentation to upper management to make someone's life a living hell.
- Work the victim's management. The stress-maker will recommend internal audits, for example, or suggest the collec-

- The victim's chair feels different but looks the same. The perpetrator swapped it out for another one of the same make and color.
- The light in the victim's office fluctuates—one day brighter . . . a few days later a little more dim. The perpetrator is changing the wattage of the light bulbs in the victim's work space.
- Things vanish and reappear the next day. The perpetrator is stealing things and returning them on a regular basis. Coffee cups are a prime example of a good target.
- The victim's nameplate is switched with someone else's or completely disappears.
- The victim's speed-dial numbers are mysteriously reprogrammed.

tion of excessive and time-consuming information with almost impossible deadlines.

- Hit a victim with more than one thing at a time. Most managers are doing well to juggle one thing at a time. Two things at a time means someone is in line for the fast track. Three things, and the manager is most likely dropping the ball on something. Thus the politico makes sure requests are always in groups of three or more.
- Recruit partners. The more people who are asking for information, the more people who are inflicting stress, the more stress will build.
- Disrupt the target's schedule. The most effective requests involve projects or analysis that require late nights, weekend

work, or other things that disrupt the normal routine. This too adds to stress and often prevents the victim from venting anxiety.

Inflicting stress requires careful management in pressing the attack. Hitting someone all at once with this is generally seen as blatant office politics, too obvious for a savvy individual. When applied gradually, slowly increasing the stress factors, the tactic is subtle and nearly impossible for a victim to notice.

Maintaining the stress levels is important for this tactic to work. If the perpetrator slackens off, the target has time to regroup, relax, and possibly counterattack. It takes a great deal of time to implement this tactic, but that's necessary for it to be fully effective.

Impact   This tactic is relatively limited to an individual or a small group working for an individual. Its effects are generally short term, if only because it requires resources (time and effort) to maintain this kind of political assault.

Politicos know that some individuals are naturally resilient when it comes to stressful situations. This limits their opportunity to apply this tactic in every case. It is best used on political adversaries that clearly do not deal well with stress.

Countermeasures   *If you are the target of this tactic . . .* you need to keep things in perspective. It's just a job. You can leave it and find another, most likely for more money. The key here is not to panic. Or better yet, if you do panic, never let it show. Don't give anyone the satisfaction of seeing you strain under the pressure.

Second, avoid all the things you can that cause stress. Eat well, get some exercise, work it off. If you don't take the time to burn off your built-up anxiety, your stress will take control of you. In terms of the workload, keep your management in the loop and establish realistic deadlines. Don't be afraid to point out that one of your peers might be deliberately trying to make *both* of you look bad with unrealistic requests and expectations. Also, you can always ask for additional help or temporary manpower to deal with elevated workloads.

Finally, don't pass on your stress to others. Like a virus, some people have stress, others are carriers. When infected, carriers tend to spread the stress to their subordinates and cause larger, more organizational problems.

If you witness this tactic being applied to your superior, mentor, or someone on your staff . . . don't be part of the problem. Take on some of the burden yourself. If possible, divert some of the workload that is causing the elevated stress levels to other staff members.

You can also retaliate with your own political counterattack. Look at the other tactics that are open to you. Find one that can tie down your opposition. Stress manipulation works if and only if it is maintained. Give the aggressor something new to worry about, and you can give yourself and your management some necessary breathing room.

Between the Sheets— Sex and the Modern Office

Let's face it, there is no equality between the sexes in the workplace. No amount of sensitivity training and sexual harassment or awareness classes can kill centuries of behavior when it

he Glass Ceiling Women have complained for decades that there is a glass ceiling that prevents their rise to upper levels of management. They are right, though in many cases the companies or firms that have such restrictions are not subtle enough to make it glass—it's concrete. Oftentimes the glass ceiling is not just for women, but for any other minority (depending on the company in question), faction, social or religious group, and so on.

And those token women who manage to penetrate to the higher ranks of management are often chosen for their ability to deal with the men in upper management, rather than for their true managerial skill.

And those who do get those jobs are almost always labeled by lower-level male managers as "the babe who slept her way to the top." So what's a working girl to do?

comes to the interactions between men and women. This is something that happens more on a genetic, instinctive level than anything else.

Sex between people in the office occurs. In fact, with a record number of females in the workforce, it is occurring with greater regularity than ever before. That is not necessarily a bad thing, despite the scorn that this author is likely to draw from every right- and left-wing women's rights group out there. In many cases, sex is discreet and happens out of love or lust rather than a quest for political power.

Sex and politics have gone hand in hand for generations as well. Remember Macbeth? As that play illustrates, a little seduction can often sway even the sternest and most loyal of people. With sex happening between co-workers, sex and

First, read the section on dealing with policies, rules, and so on, later in this chapter. Second, exploit the fact that you're female and have worked hard and gotten to the top through your merit—even if it isn't true. Third, for those who take the cheap shots on you, implying that you slept your way to the top when you didn't, persecute them. Sic the Human Resources Department on them. Given the undercurrents of political correctness that prevail in the office, you can be assured that their careers will be dragged through the mud in an effort to make sure that they do not infringe on your rights.

politics get hopelessly intertwined. Understanding these kinds of relationships is important if you hope to survive in the office. Even if you don't plan on using the bed as a springboard to a bigger office, you may find yourself bearing the brunt of someone else's political assault where sex is the weapon of choice.

Why is there so much sex in the office? People are working long hours there, in many cases spending most of their waking hours in the office rather than at home in a given week. Also, the office is often a pressure-cooker in terms of stress. Relationships are forced together because everyone has a common bond—they were all stupid enough to come work at the same place. Together these factors help forge friendships and late hours of being alone with other people.

Just to clarify matters, this is not just an issue of women sleeping with their bosses to get ahead. Traditionally this has been the case, but times are changing. With the influx of females in management positions, there is a growing number of men who are sleeping with their bosses to get ahead. *Note: This doesn't even take into account homosexuality in the office, which has a set of implications all its own.*

There are several ways that sex can come into play in the office. First is the most traditional method, sleeping with someone in upper management for favoritism. The second is a variant on the first, sleeping with someone in management and leveraging that information (Read: "blackmailing that manager") to get advancement and power in the office. The third method is implicating sexual impropriety to ruin a manager's career for personal advancement.

Sleeping with the boss: Not exactly an original idea, but this is one of the most common methods of obtaining power and position in an office.

This tactic has a strong upside for someone sleeping with a high enough level of management. Wasting time on a manager who is not on the rise or who is low in the organizational chart or pecking order does no good. The sexual partner or target should be on the fast track—not on the way out.

Another factor to consider is a simple one: How many people are in the game? If managers are willing to risk their careers by sleeping with subordinates, is it possible that they are doing the same thing with lots of subordinates? If they are, none of the sleeping partners have much chance to fully leverage this tactic. Worst-case scenario: the subordinates wind up sharing not only the bed but the power with all the other sluts or sleazes.

A truly scheming subordinate will pick a bedmate who has something to risk. A marriage, children, and so on are always a plus because they are substantial risk factors that a potential target will most likely not want to lose. Furthermore, a bedmate who is a member of a church or holder of some community position will not want to jeopardize that position by having an illicit affair exposed.

In this more traditional use of the tactic of sleeping his or her way to the top, the subordinate never needs to threaten to expose the bedmate. The fact that somebody is having this relationship in the first place is blackmail enough. The existing risk factors force the manager into a position that risks exposure and possible embarrassment (or worse).

The subordinate subtly introduces advancement plans to the bedmate, casually suggesting interest in new job positions or projects. Direct threats or coercion are not required in this relationship because it is mutually understood that this is a symbiotic relationship from the start—sex for power or position.

Blackmailing the target: Sometimes, given the personality and position of the bedmate, subordinates find it necessary to be more blunt. Blunt, in this case means a direct threat to expose this affair if political favors are not provided in return. Some call it blackmail. Others call it "opportunity knocking."

The risk factor here is high. First of all, the subordinate must be damn sure that the target will not call the card. Those who miscalculate risk losing their own careers, or at least their credibility.

Also, this escalation of matters to the point of blackmail exposes the subordinate as an individual who is performing this act solely for political advancement—a bed-hopper. Basic Rule of Sexual Blackmail: Be prepared for some degree of backlash

Word About Sexual Preferences The bitter truth is that there are individuals out there who are willing to blackmail people based on the sex of the people they are attracted to. And there are others who never use this information as blackmail but spread word through the company grapevine about a person's sexual preference.

If this information becomes publicly known, it can lead to blackballing of careers and other nasty political back-stabbing efforts. Regardless of what a company will say in its employee or policy manuals, in most companies the tag of *homosexual* is one that can bog down or ruin a career.

There are a few things that work well for non-heteros out there. One, as time passes people care less and less for

from this kind of action. The target will warn other potential victims—and the perpetrator still has to look in the mirror every morning.

Ruining careers through accusation: Companies hate messy lawsuits springing from sexual harassment cases, even if those cases have little or no bearing in reality. Some companies or firms, in an effort to protect their own reputations, will release personnel involved in such accusations. Others react by immediately relocating the accuser or accused to other departments until the matter is resolved.

When it comes to sexual impropriety, the accusation does significant political damage even if it is totally fictitious. Someone who opts to use this tactic had better do a lot of homework first to find out how the company has dealt with this kind of issue in the past. It is also essential to involve other credible individuals in this operation, dropping hints with them about

the distinction about someone's sexual preference. Two, more homosexuals are rising up the ranks of corporate management and have little tolerance for office gay-bashing.

The other thing that works to a homosexual's advantage is the fact that most companies have little formal tolerance of gay-bashing. If you can trace a rumor back to its source, or even *implied* source, it can injure, damage, or destroy that other person's career. Check with your Human Resources Department. This puts a powerful weapon in the hands of the people trying to defend themselves.

the target's harassment or exploitation. This will help support the case should it require further investigation by management.

The use of this variant tactic has a great deal of risk, but it also has great rewards. If it fails in its execution, the politico's present job is virtually destroyed. If successful, it can utterly destroy the career of the target. Even if the target stays on the job, the attack will cripple every project during the period of investigation.

Impact   Sleeping the way to the top is a rapid way to advance a career . . . that's why it has been so popular throughout history. Its time frame for success can be relatively short, three to six months.

In terms of impact, sleeping with upper management has a lot of perks and benefits associated with it. Depending on the tactical variant and the manager in question, results can be minor to major. Select projects or cherished promotions may open up if the target is at the right level and in the right position of power. Depending on how adept the horizontal politician is at pillow talk, info about upcoming management changes, personnel issues (which are good for separate leverage and blackmailing or character assassination efforts for those inclined to use them), and even the target's own political secrets may become available. Meanwhile, the only risk is personal humiliation—there is little anyone can do about promotion or information after it's obtained—unless the politician also has the risks associated with a family or outside interests.

Variants of this procedure can also be used to damage or destroy careers. A hard enough blow can shatter someone's home life, break up marriages, or drive people to financial ruin via divorce court. There is collateral damage, however, because in any accusation (whether based on reality or not) both sides will suffer the slings and arrows of the office grapevine's judgment.

Countermeasures   *If a co-worker is sleeping his or her way into a seat of power* . . . the best defense is a good offense. Some cubicle warriors will drop a hint to the target manager that they were told about the affair by members of the company grapevine, meaning that it is public knowledge. This will add stress to the entire affair, if not force it to break up entirely.

Another countertactic that works is for someone to drop word informally to Human Resources that sexual harassment is taking place in the office. This will force a flurry of informal investigation that is likely to ruin the careers of both individuals. Other inviduals will strike at the home front, calling the target's spouse . . . though this is low even for those who undertake politics for a living. Still, it is not unheard of.

Generally the best approach is to work through the manager rather than the employee. One, it places you in a power position because the implication is that you know something . . . something that the involved parties would like to keep secret. Second, you can gain advancement and benefit from the knowledge of the affair simply as a means of keeping you quiet about what you may or may not know.

If your manager is attempting to seduce you into sleeping with him or her for advancement . . . make the best moral choice. Remember, however, cool-headed cubicle warriors can inflict incredible damage in terms of blackmail and leverage with existing corporate policies regarding sexual harassment or impropriety—without having to shed a single layer of clothing.

Those who opt for the fast and easy route, sleeping with upper management, must make sure that they are doing it with the right managers—ones who can advance their careers significantly. These subordinates are taking a big risk and want to make sure it pays off!

Avoidance and the Art of the Dodge

As stated earlier, there are two concepts that are common throughout the corporate community that managers deal with every day: authority and responsibility. Managers want as much authority as possible since this is often true power (politically and otherwise) in a company.

When it comes to responsibility, however, most managers do their best to maintain their distance. Responsibility is a thing that is best dodged, avoided, or hidden from. If you have responsibility, you also carry the burdens associated with it. Thus you are saddled with having to deal with all of problems the responsibility is attached to—as well as all of the political risk.

Responsibility is one of those things that no one wants, a proverbial hot potato in an organization. Power is equated with authority, but responsibility is seen as a burden. The reality of the situation is that for every element of power that involves authority, someone must have responsibility.

The tactic commonly known as the Dodge lets you ensure that someone else gets tagged with the responsibility, while at the same time you manage to hold onto the authority yourself. More important, of all of the tactics that are outlined in this chapter, this is one of the few that is almost purely defensive in nature. It is not aimed at seizing power but maintaining it.

There is no pure blueprint for the Dodge because it is highly dependent on what it is you are striving for in terms of avoiding responsibility as well as the corporate culture and your manager's management style, but there are some guidelines you can follow. The next several paragraphs give some tips that can help you divert responsibility away from yourself while still maintaining power.

■ *You control the authority, but have someone on your staff take the responsibility.* To do this you usually need to justify that the project requires someone with special knowledge or technical skills to take final responsibility. This is common in MIS activities where someone is in charge of MIS, but another lower-level supervisor is responsible for making sure that the network or e-mail is operational.

The only drawback to this version of the tactic is that you can be injured politically by collateral damage if something does go wrong in the area where the responsibility is attached. As the manager of the person who is responsible, some of that responsibility spills over onto you no matter how much you distance yourself.

■ *Apply a matrix management structure.* Matrix management organization charts have split functional managers. Thus you may have a project manager responsible for an entire project, but a specific task may involve an individual who works in another department. For purposes of this sample project, that individual reports to the project manager, but other tasking is still handled in his or her original department.

The net result of this kind of structure is that it is hard to tell who is really in charge of what. Furthermore, the individuals trapped in such organization structures often get confusing and mixed messages about what to do and who they really report to.

As a result of matrix management, you can usually pass responsibility to other groups, thus dodging it yourself. You can convince subordinates under a matrix organization that they are responsible for some aspect of the business, and if a problem arises you can divert the blame to the parent manager rather than shoulder it yourself.

For example, say you've brought Bob from the Accounting Department into your area with responsibility for cutting purchase orders—while maintaining signing authority for yourself. If an error comes up, you don't get involved; you can pass the problem up to Bob's direct manager, Cheryl.

■ *Maintain a constant state of reorganization.* This form of the Dodge is aimed at maintaining a high enough level of confusion that no one is sure who exactly has the responsibility. In many companies where reorganization is a way of life, this version of Dodging responsibility is viable and useful.

When a problem or crisis emerges, no one can be sure who is responsible for resolving the issue.

Impact   This tactic, while primarily defensive, has moderate to low impact on your opposition. Depending on the severity of the crisis that calls responsibility into question—upper-level managers might not really care that you are trying to shrug off responsibility—you may get the responsibility associated with you despite your dodging efforts.

Countermeasures   Every time you dodge responsibility you are, in essence, placing your authority at risk. People who eventually get stuck with the responsibility often can and do make a good case for having the authority. This is often the best defense when dealing with someone executing a Dodge.

Dodging itself has some inherent risk elements. The primary risk comes from the fact that someone dodging responsibility, once identified as doing so, is seen as a weak manager who is trying to evade the obligations of the position. Most managers use this tactic, but the best counter to it is still to point out the move to upper management. Doing so injures the reputation of the individuals who are dodging and erodes their credibility with peers and superiors.

Character Assassination

> Politics ruins the character.
>
> **Otto von Bismarck**

Eroding or destroying the credibility and reliability of a political adversary is one of the more common tactics that is used in offices. It requires time and planning, but those who exercise it successfully can effectively cripple a single manager or all the information coming out of a group or department.

Character assassination requires the politician to select a target, be it a work group or a specific individual. Then, over a long period of time, it involves making sure that the credibility, accuracy, and integrity of the information coming from that target is seen by upper management as inaccurate, questionable, or unreliable.

For character assassination to work effectively it must have two pieces in place:

- Upper management must be given access to a pattern of misinformation allegedly from the target.
- Upper management must, at some point, be made aware that this misinformation is well known in the company or firm and is a character or integrity problem with the target.

These are done through a number of different approaches. There are two basic concepts that come into play with character assassination: Use the truth against someone, or use lies. Every department or group or team manager is hiding something. They are distorting or massaging figures on financial reports, concealing problem projects or even problem employees, and so on. No one is perfect. Character assassins who use the truth crank up their intelligence-gathering apparatus to learn the little hidden secrets that targets hide, then release that information to upper management. The character assassins who lie employ tactics discussed earlier in this chapter.

Obviously, character assassination makes heavy use of the corporate grapevine to slowly release information to upper management. The idea is to build a seeming pattern of falsehood and mistrust. The next key aspect of character assassination is for upper management to believe that the rest of the organization is *aware* of this series of lies perpetuated by the target department or individual. This information is important because it escalates the burden on upper management to begin questioning the integrity of *all* information coming from the target source. This element forces upper management action to avoid looking stupid . . . something that most senior managers or supervisors or VPs spend most of their careers trying to avoid.

Impact   It is important to remember that the impact of this tactic is either departmental or individual. However, when a specific individual is the assassination target, the damage is most likely to spread to that person's department.

The impact of character assassination is long-term. It can take months to perform properly, but once it is done the damage is long-lasting. Targeted departments or people have a hard time rebuilding credibility with upper management, and even if they do, the taint of their potential for misleading is still present—sometimes even after senior management changes.

Countermeasures   This is not the kind of tactic that you want to wait too long before responding to, since the damage from it can take years to clear. If you are the target (either in the department or individually), there are a few things that you can do to control the damage of an assassination attempt.

The most common counter to this is to rely on the tactic of scapegoating. Refer to that section of this chapter for further information on this approach. The scapegoat is a patsy, but the more formal the response tying the scapegoat to the smoking gun, the more credible it is in the eyes of upper management—whose respect you are fighting to maintain.

Another common defense is to accuse the character assassin of crying wolf. Every manager or department has some skeletons in its closets that it wishes would go away or stay hidden. In using a cry-wolf approach, you counterattack by going to upper management and pointing out that the individual who has targeted you is simply crying wolf—he or she is playing politics and making up wild stories. In many cases you can show that the instances in question have little true bearing on how business is done or were not significant in the first place. In some versions of this, managers open their proverbial books—so to speak. They expose everything that they have hidden in their closets so that the person sniping at them has little future ammunition.

The cry-wolf counterattack works because, if you have the rapport with upper management and execute it well, you can turn the character assassination attempt around. Instead of questioning your credibility, they begin to look at the person who was trying to smear yours.

Finally, if you are so inclined and your staff is supportive enough, you can use character assassination attempts as a common denominator to forge a team. "This could happen to you too . . . " is often enough to bring together even the most dysfunctional of organizations.

Bury Your Boss

> A cock has influence on his own dunghill.
>
> **Publilius Syrus**

Most managers want to maintain some degree of communications with their underlings; it's a normal part of business operations. Overloading their communications system can easily

he Indecisive Manager   As H. A. Hopf said, "Indecision is debilitating; it feeds upon itself; it is, one might almost say, habit-forming. Not only that, but it is contagious; it transmits itself to others."

At one point or another you will encounter the indecisive manager. They are hard to spot in a crowd, which is one reason they are not killed by the masses of employees who find themselves frustrated by these managers' lack of activity or inability to make even common-sense decisions.

Understand their motivations. They made decisions ages ago in their careers, and they got burned for it. So in order to survive, in their feeble minds, they simply do not make decisions. They stall, send the problem to committee for research or recommendation, sit on it, wait, pause, contemplate, whatever it takes to avoid making any sort of a business decision. They will want to monitor all departmental communications, editing them to make sure that nothing leaves their department or work group that might be used against them politically.

In other words, they are weak-kneed wusses; frustrating as all hell to work for or deal with.

drive your management to the brink of insanity. And given the technology in most offices, with e-mail and voice mail systems now the norm, this tactic is becoming easier than ever to execute. What makes this tactic different it is that it is aimed at burying your supervisor with communications to the point that you can pass along information that would normally cause a lot of alarm without drawing any notice. Also this tactic can

The Bury the Boss tactic is commonly used against these pillars of the corporate world to force them to make decisions. If you need management to make a decision and the manager doesn't have the guts to do it, use e-mail or voice mail to do it for them. A typical version of such a message would be as follows:

"If I do not receive a response from you in the next 48 hours on the above subject matter, I will assume that you concur with my stand on this issue."

What this does is force the individual to either make a decision on the matter or make a de facto decision by doing nothing at all—which the procrastinator is best at. Keeping quiet feels like it maintains plausible deniability over the matter—if anything goes wrong, the manager will claim the message never arrived in the first place. If you try this ploy, make sure you maintain a copy of the information you send and any or all confirmations that the message was opened by your lily-livered manager.

be used to smuggle in the boss's agreement or compliance with some practice, change in operation or process, and so on, all apparently with their full knowledge—since no mortal human being can master two persons' worth of e-mail and voice mail and do it effectively.

Burying your boss can be done easily under the guise of "keeping you in the loop" in terms of projects that your

hat Makes a Good Status Report? Status reports are how management either (a) knows what's going on or (b) wastes reams of paper annually. If you are going to actually use performance management techniques, you need to make sure you can get to information quickly and easily—and a status report is the best way to see what your staff is working on (or lying about).

The following are suggested elements of a good status report format that managers should require from their subordinates:

- *Annual Goals Status.* This is the stuff that performance reviews are made of. You did give your staff annual goals, right? Staff should list the goal, the latest work completed, and the due date.

supervisor may have some interest in. With managers who tend to micromanage, this is even easier to accomplish—they are constantly requiring information and updates anyway (whether they read the stuff or not is irrelevant).

In the process of forwarding your communications to your supervisor, you can sneak in a wide range of information. Bad news, for example, gets buried in the mundane notes you are forwarding. Even irate client phone calls get passed by as your boss struggles to find a way to simply get through all of the raw information and meaningless data that you are passing along every hour on the hour.

To execute the tactic, you need minimal technical skill. The key is to master two functions: forwarding e-mail and forwarding voice mail. Usually these can be done with a few

- *Project Status.* These are the projects you heaped on your staff, which is one of the reasons that they never manage to complete their annual goals. Staff should list the projects, the latest work completed, and the due dates.
- *Green Lights.* Stuff that the staff has completed in terms of projects, kudos from clients, or, in general, things that went right or as planned.
- *Yellow Lights.* This is an alert to management of things that may go wrong and blow up in their face. In other words, "Manager, I need your help to prevent these things from exploding."
- *Red Lights.* Too late! These things have exploded or are about to.

key or phone number punches. It is also necessary to add to the messages the reason that you are forwarding them to your supervisor. In most circumstances this is a notation about the project, operation, client, or other peer that this message applies to.

Rather than be totally obvious with this tactic, you should forward messages to other appropriate managers and copy your own boss. Again, it is only proper to provide some sort of explanation as to why you are copying your boss on e-mail messages. The more sinister of you out there have already leaped ahead to the assumption that yes, you can do this as a separate mail message—further adding to the burden.

The information you are sending to cover your own butt or place blame for a mistake on someone else should be sent in the same frank and candid format. This way the bad news is buried in with all the other information.

Impact   This tactic can be used both long and short term and is quick and easy to implement. The overall impact is rather limited to your manager or the next level up, depending on how you execute the tactic.

Burying a manager tends to inflict some parallel damage as well. Managers who are totally hip-deep in work tend to drop some issues. They tend to make more mistakes and use poor judgment since they don't have the time to think things through. You should keep this in mind when you are executing this tactic.

Countermeasures   The only reason you'd have to counter-attack against this tactic is if you are the victim of it . . . with one of your underlings attempting to swamp you with communications. The most obvious reaction if you are being buried under a heap of e-mail or voice mail messages is to tell the subordinate employee to stop. This is *not* the best response, however. In fact, it gives your employee permission to cut off any and all communication, make decisions without your input, and then claim that you gave the order to keep you in the dark.

The best defense against this is to manage the situation. Give the employee guidelines as to what to send and copy you on and what is simply part of the job you've assigned. Using this technique, you've put the burden of managing communications back in the hands of the employee. If someone attempts to circumvent you or start this tactic again, you can turn in a blistering performance review—with perfect justification.

Scapegoats and Sacrificial Lambs

When something goes wrong, management always looks for someone to blame. Even if it is an act of nature, someone's head has to roll. In the backstabbing world of corporate politics, this grim reality is lived out every day. Scapegoatting is one of the most common defensive political tactics you are likely to encounter.

Many managers deal with politicking through the use of a scapegoat—a sacrificial lamb, patsy, fall-guy/gal, dead man walking, road kill, memo martyr, or any other set of names known in the corporate world. These people, out of the ranks of the mindless slugs, have but one role on a project—to take the bullet meant for you or one of the more valued members of your team. Whether they like it or not, the scapegoats have the responsibility of throwing themselves on the hand grenade that would kill you. And if they don't jump at the chance, your job, as the manager, is to push or shove them onto that grenade and hold them down until it goes off.

After all, it's either you or them.

A sacrificial lamb exists to take the blame for problems or failures instead of blame falling on your department or team or even you personally. The scapegoat is usually innocent but is set up by the target or the department manager to take the brunt of the blame for the problems. Sad, but this is cubicle warfare and innocents are always the victims. Punishment of the scapegoat is done formally through official channels in most cases, including things such as HR reprimands, performance management discipline, and so on.

Most times scapegoats do not know that they have been set up in the first place. The setup gets done in the background, usually covertly. When the proverbial bomb does explode, it is not uncommon for the manager who set up the scapegoats to be the first one to tell them that they were screwed over and may even go so far as to promise go to bat for them.

When you set up scapegoats, the process begins early in the life cycle of a project. Usually more than one person gets tagged as a potential scapegoat—so if one scapegoat manages to dodge the bullet, the second one in line is taken out rather than you.

The best scapegoats that you can find in the universe are those who do not report to you directly. These types of patsies require a great deal more documentation than those whom you set up in your own organization. Where you can easily falsify documentation to set up someone in your own department or team, it is not so easy with those who don't work for you. You often have to imply through formal communications channels that these other individuals have responsibility for your critical project areas.

Scapegoats have no voice in the corporate world. They are labeled as victims and failures after the deed is done. Even during the execution of this tactic, their rebuttals to the acts they are falsely accused of fall on deaf ears.

Impact   Minimal. This being a highly defensive tactic, all setting up a scapegoat does is ensure that you personally do not get blamed for project failures or business mistakes.

It is important to note that this tactic can backfire on you as a manager if you are not careful. Some of your political opposition can call into question the fact that if the scapegoats are in your organization and you are their manager, then you, as a result, are responsible for their actions.

Countermeasures   If someone is marking you a potential scapegoat, or if you even suspect it, the time to act is before the shit hits the fan. Let management know that you are aware that someone is setting you up to take a fall. Be blunt and direct if that is your style, or let the information leak up via the grapevine. Make it clear that you are maintaining the appropriate documentation to support your true standing on the project or assignment in question. While this will not stop all attempts at scapegoating, you will find that most managers tend to pick victims who will take it quietly so as to not draw attention to them in the process. This may force the manager to seek another one of your peers as a target.

Corrupting and Contorting Company Resources, Procedures, and Political Correctness

> The more corrupt the state, the more numerous the laws.
>
> **Tacitus**

> There is only one way to fight a
> bureaucracy: with another bureaucracy.
>
> **Anonymous**

When you get a group of people together they begin to formulate procedures for how to interact. This is usually because at least one of them doesn't have enough work to do. They come up with these processes and inevitably put them in writing. This pamphlet grows until it fills a binder. The binder then gets copied, circulated, and constantly updated. Some Einstein gets the idea that putting the 500-page book online will save time and effort. This only forces people to print it out and since they all do it at different times, they all have different versions—none of which is right.

This is how policy manuals are born.

And in this day where political correctness dominates and the rules governing employees are massive tomes larger than Gutenberg Bibles, politicians lurk, waiting to exploit these rules and procedures. Like the tax code, there are numerous loopholes and gaps in the rules that indiscriminate managers should feel free to capitalize on.

The heart and soul of this tactic is to manipulate the company's policies and procedures against foes around the office. The politician finds the seemingly minor company or firm rules and contorts them as needed. If things mysteriously start to go wrong, chances are somebody is working the system against you.

Examples of this include such ploys as:

- Using friends in Purchasing, Accounting, and so on to hold up paperwork needed for a political foe's project.
- Dropping an anonymous hint with the HR department that someone in the opposition's team or group or department may be sleeping around, exploiting minorities, a closet racist, or stealing funds from the company. *Note: Almost always these rumors don't require solid details to initiate an investigation—depending on the size of the company.*

- Suggesting that a new project get assigned to someone at the same time the annual performance reviews are due—purely so as to entomb the poor bastard with work.

- Using the suggestion box (yes, there still are some out there gathering dust) to hint to management about "improprieties" in terms of an enemy's budgetary expenditures and so on. Suggesting an internal audit can tie up an office for weeks.

- Letting word out on the grapevine that a political opponent is using nepotism in hiring, bringing in old friends and relatives rather than hiring on merit.

- Suggesting that an opponent is using company computers for personal business. Policies in every company forbid this. If these rules were followed there would be no bowling scores ever posted. Likewise the use of the Internet for private use is usually banned, but at the same time estimates range that 50 percent to 70 percent of Web access by corporations is done for private use. This is a simple policy to turn and use against a fellow employee or political contender.

The nauseating waves of political correctness that have swept the corporate world have also been carried by many companies to extremes that a politician can use as a weapon. Where five years ago simple jokes in the hall would have been the norm, now even tame jokes offend someone. A politician can exploit almost any offhand comment or casual gesture by an opponent by implying to upper management or HR that there is a risk of lawsuit from such comments or activities.

A final variation of this tactic is the corruption of procedures. In this, friends, allies, and contacts are used to manipulate processes. If enemies need things from procurement,

he Stall One of the variants of this tactic is the Stall, and it is highly effective. This is where an individual uses the known processes and procedures to grind business to a halt. In this variant, the executing individual leverages political favors, friendships, or blackmailing information to slow down subsidiary processes. Some of these processes might include, but are not limited to, MIS support, purchasing, copy-room activity, secretarial pool availability, and so on.

The cubicle warrior leverages his or her contacts to strangle (stall) requests opponents make in these areas.

they may find their requests at the bottom of the pile, lost in the interoffice mail, or sent back for more supporting detail. *Note: This example is only one of hundreds of possible variations.*

Impact This corruption of company policies and guidelines has limited impact. At best it can drain company resources and keep an opponent reeling from damage and lost time. If done discretely enough, the trail leading to who initiated the assault will be almost impossible to trace.

While it has some short-term benefits, its overall impact is minimal. However, if a short-term disaster is what is sought, this is a viable tactic.

Countermeasures Every good bureaucracy has pointless rules that others exploit—that is the basis of this tactic. The bureaucracy also has procedures in place for dealing with charges, slow-downs, investigations, and so on. Many of these

Purchase requisitions get lost in the Stall. The copy room moves jobs to the bottom of the pile and loses the "rush job" label; MIS makes sure that requests for hardware get filled with 386 systems with 2 MB of RAM.

While these seem like minor irritants, in a world where speed is of the essence and many departments or groups are dependent on each other for support, this kind of tactic can frustrate and infuriate a political enemy.

are straightforward and if you know your policies well enough, you will find some degree of protection in these.

Obviously the other best counter to this tactic is to run your business in an honest, straightforward manner. Do nothing wrong, and any probing on the part of your foes will only serve to damage *their* credibility.

Hamstringing Operations: Stealing People

The cemeteries are filled with people who thought that the world couldn't get along without them.

Anonymous

No matter how much technology you have in place, when all is said and done, people are what make an organization function. People perform work. People think. People are productive. People manage. Well, not all of them.

Actually, only about 10 percent of the people fall into this category. The rest are simply there to occupy space, fill slots on an org chart, and collect paychecks. But this 10 percent of the people—the real doers, the true brains and operators of the business—are worth a fortune. Without them, nothing else really gets done. Employees in this select cadre are critical, due to their technical or specialty skills or their ability to manage, plan, or lead.

The tactic of hamstringing is where you do one of two things to your political enemies' key people. You either convince them to leave the company or firm, or convince them to come and work for you. Either way you are essentially taking away key building blocks in your political opposition's organization in an effort to watch that group or department come tumbling down.

Keep a few things in mind. Why do employees leave or change jobs? Usually it is because of money, climate or culture of the organization, or benefits. You usually can't do a blasted thing about bennies, but you can entice using money and culture. This will factor in later when you move in for the proverbial kill.

The first step in this tactic is to identify the critical personnel who are holding things together for the target department or manager. Oftentimes these are easy to spot because of their backgrounds in rare technical areas, but it may require you to do some research to determine who is making how much money. While they may not be the most highly paid members of the team, they are in the top 25 percent in most cases.

Another method is to ask yourself how easy is it to replace each person in that organization. Depending on the department, region of the country, and required skill set, this information will often help you target the critical path members.

After you find out who the key members are, you must then decide your overall approach. Are you looking to have them leave the company, or can you entice them to come and work in your group? If you get them to leave the company or firm, you are inflicting the most direct damage to the target manager or group since it then is impossible for that manager to get in contact with these people for ongoing support in their vital area. This cuts the umbilical cord, leaving your target high and dry.

Getting someone to leave the target group and join your organization has some side benefits that come into play. Chances are your targeted manager can convince upper management to force you to give some time to help any transitions, but you then are assuming control, from a power standpoint, of that aspect of the project. Also you gain the benefit of now having a person in your organization who might be able to tell you everything going on with the former supervisor and department. The skeletons that this person is aware of suddenly are placed within your grasp, which you can further leverage for political action in the future.

The next step is the execution of the hamstringing. There are many ways to entice an employee to leave a current position, no matter what the job and where it is. The following list is simply a rough guideline of some of the concepts that you can modify and use to your own devious means:

■ Tell target employees that they are woefully underpaid. Everybody is and no one likes being reminded of it. Point out classified ads to show what their peers are making. This entices the employee to either get more money (further damaging the budget of your opposition) or to look for work elsewhere.

he Art of Sabotage There is a variant of the ham-stringing tactic that is best described as sabotage. In this variant—used by politicos with strong stomachs and no scruples—rather than using people to slow down the processes or procedures to gum up the works, the idea is to hamstring an operation by sabotaging its infrastructure directly.

Sabotage happens more often than people will admit. Given the advances in technology there are numerous ways to slow up processes, screw up meetings, or simply make projects a living hell for those working on them. Some of the more common methods include:

- Removing projection panels or overhead projector light bulbs—enough to end many meetings.
- Stealing all the erasable markers from white boards (or switching them with permanent markers).

- Post employees' names with head hunters or on the Internet with job services. Calls with job offers will start rolling in—and sooner or later someone will jump at the bait.
- Take target employees to lunch. Let them know that you realize how important they are. Covertly let them know of positions you have open in your organization . . . for more money, of course.
- Use the grapevine to leak to an employee that he or she is being made a scapegoat for whatever project they may be working on. This causes friction with the supervisor even if it isn't true.
- Reward your employees—and make it known. Doing simple kinds of awards and recognitions costs little and does a

- Damaging network cables to ruin connectivity. The same can be done with fax machine phone lines and so on.
- Hiding or stealing all the toner for a copier, or shipping all the paper to another location.
- Damaging a key computer hard drive on a project. (As noted earlier, a magnet and a PC simply do not mix.)
- Stealing, shredding, or hiding key documentation such as purchase orders or requisitions, requests for supplies, and so on.

While all of these are of low ethics and high ferocity, they all have the desired impact of handicapping day-to-day operations of a group or injuring a specific event such as a training session or an important meeting.

lot for the corporate culture and your own image as a manager. You want people to want to work for you, so show that you are caring.

- Use an intermediary. Have a co-worker feel out target employees to see what they are looking for. You can also use this intermediary or stooge to plant the word with the targets about how great you are to work for.

Impact Hamstringing a project can slow or totally stop it. No one is indispensable, but while you can replace skills, you cannot replace office experience. Remove one or more of the key players, and a project can fall totally apart.

Countermeasures   If you are the target of hamstringing as a manager (that is, someone is trying to steal or drive off *your* key people), you can take a proactive approach. Reward your staff, be a real manager for a while. Make sure that your staff is getting the appropriate reinforcing praise that makes them like working there and for you. If your people are up for raises or bonuses, push to get them through. This is relatively little work compared with having to replace someone on your staff—especially one of your top performers.

If you are yourself being seduced by the dark side of corporate politics, being lured into a hamstringing effort—happy days! You are in a unique position where you can play off the two managers, having them bid against each other. It is hard to lose in this position. Don't get so greedy that an upper-level manager is forced to get involved, but for the most part, set your goals high . . . very high!

The Frontal Assault

> No poor bastard ever won a war dying for his country.
> He won it by making some other dumb bastard die for his.
>
> **General George S. Patton**

It has been said that the end move in politics is to pick up the gun. As you have seen throughout this chapter, most political tactics are done subtly, covertly, rarely in the open. This tactic is the exception to that principle. This tactic essentially is waging all-out visible political war against your enemies.

No quarter asked. No quarter given. As the saying goes, "Kill 'em all and let God sort 'em out."

When you execute this tactic, you declare open war with your enemy. This is rare, but it does happen. You let someone know what you are willing to stoop to, in public if you so choose. There is no mistake between the two of you, this is an affirmation of your understanding—that this is a fight to the bitter end.

Why be so open and blunt? Some individuals who take part in office backstabbing and politics do so because it is a nameless and faceless profession. They do not worry much about direct confrontations because they are so rare. The use of a frontal assault catches many people off guard. It pulls the veneer off the back-room politics, lays the raw innards on the table, and in the process tends to make everyone very nervous. The use of the frontal assault can break the nerves of all but the most savvy and strong-willed political boss.

When executing this tactic, you do not play all your cards. You simply make it known to your enemies that you are coming at them, and that you could come from any angle. The use of paranoia is fully authorized in the frontal assault. In some instances it is appropriate (and entertaining) to imply that you have the goods on your foe, that you know what they are up to—without, of course, saying what that is—if for nothing else than to panic them even more.

The principles at work in the frontal assault are sheer confidence and momentum. You are moving forward, directly at your enemies, in the open. The assumption is that you have more than a few cards up your sleeve. Your open declaration of war is designed, on its own, to move your enemies, to shake their spirit. As you press further, using other tactics, they will see that this is blatant and directed, and will recoil even more. Momentum will take its toll.

That's not to say that this tactic is without risks. There is little chance of mending fences after war is declared. Even years down the road, things will never be cordial between you and your foe. And your staff will be drawn into the fray—openly. Your position is a public one, you are going to take this person down. Your staff knows that they will be drawn into the fight, meaning that either they will become nervous and disheartened, or galvanized behind you in your efforts—if the cause is a just one.

Impact   This is a do-or-die option aimed specifically at removing another manager or peer, period. If you fail, you are seen as a failure by everyone. If you succeed, few will risk taking you on knowing what you are capable of. Frontal assault is a win-or-lose tactic with big stakes, your career and the career of the person you are trying to take out. One or the other will lose face or have to move on to another company or firm.

Countermeasures   So someone's declared war on you. Your options are limited. You can return the favor and open your own assault on the initiator of the attack. If the attack is mere bravado on the part of your enemy, this will potentially stop it cold.

The other option for dealing with a frontal assault is to ask for third-party arbitration. Rather than lower yourself to the level of the person declaring war on you, ask an upper-level manager or HR to intervene—to try and bring the problem issues to resolution. It's not that you really want to end the fight, but this action makes you look like the reasonable person in the matter while the attacker looks like a rabid dog frothing at the mouth. This action can be important in the future should your enemy spring more political traps for you—it will look to everyone at that point as if the attacker is being childish and immature.

Finally, outright and open cubicle warfare serves the purpose of bringing together teams. If you are under attack, you can leverage this assault to bring your organization together as a team. You can twist an open declaration of political war as a chance to make your enemy face an army rather than an individual (you).

7

How can I lose to such an idiot?

Chess Master Aaron Nimzovich

THE FACE OF THE ENEMY

This chapter deals with the types of individuals who are the soldiers of the cubicle wars raging in your office. Chances are the faces and descriptions are familiar to you, but no real names are given to protect the guilty. In a fight like this, knowing the enemy is an important part of surviving the wars.

INTRO TO THE ARCHETYPES

For each of the archetypes (also referred to as personas) provided, detailed descriptions are given. The characteristics and personality sections enable you to identify these "characters" at a distance. The age factor alerts you to the different personas lurking among Generation Xers as well as the toupee-topped crowd.

Various comments regarding politics that you might hear from such personas are presented in case you happen to overhear a conversation while at the water fountain. Like signposts, the words we say help identify us, even in a crowd. In this case, the quotes provided also give you some insight into the personalities of individuals you may face in the office.

Veteran and novice cubicle warriors will also want to read through the Tactics Favored section for each of the archetypes. This tells you not only what they will do (in general), but what works against them. In this type of warfare, information is ammo for your own defense.

Aggressors

These politicians are major players in the game known as cubicle warfare. They've been there and done that—and have the scars to prove it. Their careers were forged not by hard work, though there were rumors of that in the past, but rather by taking part in office politics. Aggressors have been playing the game so long that they cannot distinguish it from their job. Politics is what they do for a living.

Every major committee and policy group has them on the membership rolls. Upper management knows them by name—and knows they are so close to achieving that level they can smell the executive washrooms. They share a disdain for their own managers, not really caring for them and seeing them as what is holding them back from an office on mahogany row.

Bottom line with Aggressors: they will shed all the blood necessary to achieve their career goals, regardless of what it does to their reputation or how they look in the eyes of others. The higher the body count along the way, the better.

Age   32+

Comments Regarding Politics   "I don't play politics, it's too nasty. You mess with me though, and I'll take you down."

"Sure there's some backstabbing that's taken place, but that's all just part of being in business."

Political Tendencies   Aggressors live for politics as a way to achieve their goals and objectives. In their minds they know that they are playing politics, but they never say so out loud. To them, they are the masters of the game. Their peers are other Aggressors, mostly because they do not want to associate with people who are not cut from the same cloth.

Sometimes this rush of egotism gets them into trouble. They get a Teflon feeling, that what their actions have no consequences and that they cannot be hurt. Sometimes, usually while still in their 30s, most Aggressors take a serious hit politically to knock some sense into them. They tend to play the game still, just a little more conservatively.

Tactics Favored   The tactics that you are likely to see Aggressors deploy are some variation of the following:

> Lower the River
> Lying
> Bypass
> Death by Committee
> Riding the Craze du Jour
> Avoidance and Dodging
> Character Assassination
> Scapegoating

Corrupting Resources, Procedures, and Policies

Hamstringing Operations

Susceptible To   If you are facing an Aggressor, the best tactics to use are as follows:

Brownnosing

Lying

Bypass

Death by Committee

Stress Manipulation

Between the Sheets

Bury Your Boss

Hamstringing Operations

Frontal Assault

Hoppers

Corporate politicians of this type are constant job changers. They do this to avoid having their mistakes catch up with them. With many of these individuals, it can be hard to tell that they are hopping until you take a long, serious look at their career paths. One thing they are smooth at is making themselves look stable while changing jobs like underwear.

The reason that they change jobs is that they burn their bridges with each new manager because of the poor way that they wage office politics. Rather than take a stand, they keep on the move. Rather than deal with the consequences of bad political tactics execution, they move. The only thing that everyone concurs with is that every time they move, they manage to make more money or get a better position out of the deal.

Age   25 to 35

Comments Regarding Politics   "There have been politics in every place that I've worked. That's why I left my last job . . . and the one before that. I don't take part in the politics, it just seems to follow me."

"Politics? Not me. . . ."

"If you think this place is bad, you should've seen the last place I worked."

Political Tendencies   Hoppers are the classic sloppy politicians. They need this book and a dollop of common sense if they hope to survive. They know that the way to get ahead in the company or firm is to be a player in the cubicle warfare games raging around them. But they tend to rush in, make mistakes, and not deal well with their failures. When everything comes rushing in at them, they run and hide rather than deal with it.

Remember, Hoppers always believe that the grass is greener somewhere else. They refuse to believe that they play politics badly, it's just they've been set up—in their minds anyway.

After several years of this running and hiding, these individuals either develop some acumen and evolve into another persona, or they tick someone off to the point that they are the target of such a vicious political attack that they are driven from the company in disgrace.

If people on a Hopper's staff get involved in politics, they generally have to sink or swim on their own. Survival of the fittest tends to be the motivator for the Hopper as manager.

Tactics Favored   The tactics that you are likely to see a Hopper deploy are some variation of the following:

Brownnosing

Lying

Bypass

Riding the Craze du Jour

Between the Sheets

Avoidance and Dodging

Bury Your Boss

Scapegoating

Susceptible To   If you are facing a Hopper, the best tactics to use are as follows:

Lower the River

Lying

Death by Committee

Character Assassination

Frontal Assault

Survivalists

As politicians, Survivalists count on outlasting their political enemies rather than defeating them in a prolonged battle. They concentrate on surviving as opposed to getting into a stand-up fight with a true victory. Survivalists love reorganization because it gives them a chance to be forgotten by the political animals stalking the halls.

Survivalists are often former political players who fell from grace. They may have been scapegoats on a failed program or project. They enter this survival mode because they feel that they can ill afford to have to start looking for a new job or to start a new career. Nothing would make them happier than to escape political death long enough to reach retirement.

Age   40+

Comments Regarding Politics   "If you want to play politics, fine, just don't get me involved."

"I've seen too many careers go up in flames over stupid political games."

Political Tendencies   Survivalists do everything they can to stay out the line of fire when it comes to cubicle warfare. They hate working for political managers and every time they see a political storm brewing, they retreat to the safety of their cubicles in hopes that it will pass them.

If they play politics at all, they do it solely in an attempt to survive, rarely to prosper.

Tactics Favored   The tactics that you are likely to see the Survivalist deploy are some variation of the following:

> Brownnosing
> Avoidance and Dodging
> Scapegoating

Susceptible To   If you are facing a Survivalist, the best tactics to use are as follows:

> Lower the River
> Lying
> Stress Manipulation
> Between the Sheets
> Character Assassination
> Bury Your Boss
> Scapegoating

Corrupting Resources, Procedures, and Policies
Frontal Assault

Career Politicians

Like Aggressors, people matching this archetype are known throughout the company or firm as vigorous cubicle warriors. The difference is that while Aggressors play politics to achieve specific goals and objectives, Career Politicians have roles in the political arena to the point that playing politics is their career.

These sick puppies get a chuckle out of the havoc that they wreak. They lack guilt to the point that some might consider them sociopathic, yet they are so highly personable that no one really suspects they are insane.

Career Politicians have no friends, lots of enemies, and a large contingency of people who just fear them. They commonly host power lunches and dinner meetings. Work is everything to them—and work for them is the political games that they play.

Age   35+

Comments Regarding Politics   "Good politics is what made this company what it is today."

"You see this as someone playing politics. Hell, I'm just trying to do my job as best I can."

Political Tendencies   Aggressive. Like hungry sharks, Career Politicians spend a lot of time sizing up everyone in the company in terms of what they can provide or what kind of threat they might pose either now or down the road. To people with this persona, everyone is the next potential meal.

They are aware of the fact that they are taking part in the game of cubicle warfare, but at the same time they are somewhat in denial about the damage that they cause. To them it is a flexing of power, regardless of what it does to other's careers and livelihoods.

Career Politicians are somewhat paranoid, to the point that they tend to lead with an attack rather than wait for themselves to be a target.

Tactics Favored   The tactics that you are likely to see the Career Politician deploy are some variation of the following:

> Lying
> Riding the Craze du Jour
> Stress Manipulation
> Between the Sheets
> Character Assassination
> Scapegoating
> Corrupting Resources, Procedures, and Policies
> Hamstringing Operations
> Frontal Assault

Susceptible To   If you are facing a Career Politician, the best tactics to use are as follows:

> Brownnosing
> Bypass
> Death by Committee
> Riding the Craze du Jour
> Stress Manipulation
> Between the Sheets

Bury Your Boss

Corrupting Resources, Procedures, and Policies

Hamstringing Operations

Frontal Assault *(but only if you are sure you have the upper hand from start to finish)*

Apoliticals

Apoliticals operate above and below the political delimiter. They do not take part in petty cubicle wars, but also know enough about politics to get the work done regardless.

The problem people who fit the Apolitical archetype pose is that they are hard to corrupt. This is because they generally have a high self-confidence, few skeletons in their closet, and when pressed will take the moral high ground, muddying any politico who tries to take them on.

This is not to say that they will not take part in politics altogether, but when they do, they do so for their own moral reasons and rarely for personal gain. These individuals are hard for normal cubicle warriors to deal with because they don't panic and are strong willed. *(Think of the younger Oliver North or G. Gordon Liddy and you are pretty much on target.)*

Age   25+

Comments Regarding Politics   "Politics is sometimes a necessary evil—but it's always evil."

"I only do what is necessary for the success of the organization, not for my own profit."

Political Tendencies   When they are not taking part in politics, these people are dormant and virtually immune to cubicle warfare tactics because warfare simply does not appeal to them. They react when messed with, and react in a way that you will not like.

When they are politically active they are Aggressors to the extreme. There are few limits to their actions, and they tend to take on even the strongest political bosses or career politicians.

Tactics Favored   The tactics that you are likely to see Apoliticals deploy are some variation of the following:

Lying
Bypass
Stress Manipulation
Bury Your Boss
Scapegoating
Corrupting Resources, Procedures, and Policies
Hamstringing Operations
Frontal Assault

Susceptible To   If you are facing an Apolitical persona, the best tactics to use are as follows:

Lower the River
Bypass
Death by Committee
Riding the Craze du Jour
Avoidance and Dodging

Bosses

This is a role similar to that of a crime family leader. Bosses don't play politics obviously—they manipulate others into doing it for them. They have several other managers or employees who work in their organization who are all able and apt cubicle warriors. In their political dealings, Bosses spend most of their time holding court with their underlings, helping them plan their own tactics and strategies.

Bosses have been around the block and know the way that the war is waged. Rather than concentrate on their own career, they look at forging empires. Their empires are beyond organization charts and are built on real power, not pieces of paper. Bosses view things in perspective from the big picture.

Age   35+

Comments Regarding Politics   "One day, and that day may never come, I may ask you to do a favor for me."

"You are more than a member of my staff, you are family. We take care of family."

Political Tendencies   Bosses are well insulated from the backstabbing and cutthroat behavior of the office; they tend to leave their followers to deal with this. Unlike some of the archetypes, they don't abandon their staff when they run into trouble, but instead bail them out. This forges a sense of loyalty and allows their underlings to be willing to take bigger risks for higher stakes in the Boss's battles.

Bosses work with honor almost as deep as that of the Apolitical persona. They do not stoop personally to underhanded approaches, but they are willing to allow those who work for them to do so.

Above all, Bosses leverage political favors from their underlings or peers. They ask for favors and expect them filled— either now or down the road.

Tactics Favored   The tactics that you are likely to see Bosses deploy are some variation of the following:

> Bypass
> Death by Committee
> Riding the Craze du Jour
> Between the Sheets
> Avoidance and Dodging
> Hamstringing Operations
> Frontal Assault

Susceptible To   If you are facing a Boss figure, the best tactics to use are as follows:

> Brownnosing
> Bypass
> Between the Sheets
> Bury Your Boss

Mindless Slugs

Mindless Slugs account for a large number of the population of most corporations or firms. These are the rank and file who know that cubicle warfare is out there and pray nightly that it does not get near them. Usually these prayers are pointless, but they do help them sleep.

The Mindless Slugs are the victims, the sheep with the cubicle warriors playing the roles of wolves. They don't have the guts to be take a risk in office politics, but at the same time live in fear of being sucked into a political game—and they often bear the brunt of the warfare that is fought in the offices.

Two words: cannon fodder.

Age   22+

Comments Regarding Politics   "Do what you want to my supervisor, just let me go!"

"Please spare me, I have a wife and children."

"I'm not a wuss, I just don't want to end up like the others."

Political Tendencies   The Mindless Slugs of the universe cower at the mere mention of the words *office politics*. Anything they do is defensive in nature, never offensive lest they draw attention and fire from the real political players. Mindless Slugs have but one purpose: to act as chud for the sharks swimming in the organization where they work.

Tactics Favored   The tactics that you are likely to see Mindless Slugs deploy are some variation of the following:

> Death by Committee
> Avoidance and Dodging

Susceptible To   If you are facing a Mindless Slug, the best tactics to use are as follows:

> Brownnosing
> Lower the River
> Lying
> Bypass
> Death by Committee
> Riding the Craze du Jour
> Stress Manipulation

Between the Sheets
Avoidance and Dodging
Character Assassination
Bury Your Boss
Scapegoating
Corrupting Resources, Procedures, and Policies
Hamstringing Operations
The Frontal Assault

Hell, they all apply. Dealing with this archetype is roughly akin to shooting fish in a barrel. There is no real competition or risk in trying anything.

TESTING YOURSELF: WHO ARE YOU?

It's very hard to say what kind of politician a person is since personality figures in greatly. One way you can identify what persona best exemplifies you is to simply read the descriptions and pick the one that sounds most like you. In all honesty, this is probably the most accurate methodology.

The problem that you run into with the archetypes is that they tend to blur. An Aggressor and a Boss for example have some similar tendencies, and it is difficult to tell where one ends and the next begins. That's okay; throughout your career, you may move through three or more of these personas, evolving (or is it devolving?) as your career and your experience in internal office politics develop.

For those out there who want to determine what they are most prone to, we need to expand on the test you took back in Chapter 3, factoring in your preferences in tactics. It is important to note that this may only point to tendencies in terms of

eneration X in the Workplace   In 1962 or 1963 the Baby Boomer period came to an end and a new era, the age of Generation X, came into being. As these individuals enter the workforce they are having an impact on office politics that is unique and may force a new evolution in cubicle warfare, an escalation of the ongoing wars that have been fought for the last few decades in every office.

There are some factors that Generation X brings into the office that will influence politics as it is played. These are . . .

- *Egos.* This generation feels that they are owed something just for having been born. Egos tend to feed cubicle warfare, which means that as this generation becomes more politically savvy, the tactics used are going to be more of a cutthroat nature. In the short term, this leads to them being more willing to take part in politics in the office simply to have a place in the game.
- *No Loyalty.* Gen X folks will hop jobs in a heartbeat. They saw their parents get laid off in the '60s and '70s and don't share their parents misplaced loyalty in companies or firms. The age of the "organization man" has come to an end.
- *Aggressive.* Combined with their hefty egos, Generation Xers are almost blindly aggressive—they figure they have little to lose and everything to gain. Despite

the archetypes. When all is said and done, your own personality really will determine which of these personas (or combination of the several) best fits you personally.

For each of the tactics listed, rate your willingness to use that tactic in your dealings with cubicle warfare. A rating of 1

the age of political correctness, they will undertake any and all tactics even early in their careers.

- ■ *Rules Driven.* This generation has a love of rules. They want job descriptions as a means of protection. They are used to rules and guidelines because they have governed their personal lives, and they rely on rules in the office. They know how to use the rules and policies to their advantage (after years of watching Mom and Dad cheat on their taxes) and are masters at finding loopholes in policies or using them as weapons (Corrupting Resources, Procedures, and Policies).
- ■ *Litigious.* They love to sue companies. Baby Boomers don't hold a candle to Generation X when it comes to filing law suits for harassment or discrimination. They learned the rules and exploit them, regardless of the long-term consequences.

Older corporate politicians and seasoned cubicle warfare veterans will find this group as easy to kill as cockroaches—and hard to deal with as cornered rats. They are filled with paradox. Many are willing to sleep their way to the top, but at the same time they are the number-one group to file sexual harassment charges. One thing is for sure, their impact in the workplace as a whole is one that is likely to have long-range implications—and the same is true in the world of cubicle warfare.

indicates that you would not be willing to use the tactic at all. A 5 rating would indicate that, if the circumstances were right, you might consider using that tactic. A rating of 10 indicates that this is something you are using right now or have used recently and would be willing to do it again.

Rating the Tactics

1. Brownnosing

| 1 | 2 | 3 | 4 | 5 | 6 | 7 | 8 | 9 | 10 |

2. Avoidance and Dodging

| 1 | 2 | 3 | 4 | 5 | 6 | 7 | 8 | 9 | 10 |

3. Scapegoating

| 1 | 2 | 3 | 4 | 5 | 6 | 7 | 8 | 9 | 10 |

4. Bypass

| 1 | 2 | 3 | 4 | 5 | 6 | 7 | 8 | 9 | 10 |

5. Bury Your Boss

| 1 | 2 | 3 | 4 | 5 | 6 | 7 | 8 | 9 | 10 |

6. Corrupting Resources, Procedures, and Policies

| 1 | 2 | 3 | 4 | 5 | 6 | 7 | 8 | 9 | 10 |

7. Lower the River

| 1 | 2 | 3 | 4 | 5 | 6 | 7 | 8 | 9 | 10 |

8. Death by Committee

| 1 | 2 | 3 | 4 | 5 | 6 | 7 | 8 | 9 | 10 |

9. Hamstringing Operations

| 1 | 2 | 3 | 4 | 5 | 6 | 7 | 8 | 9 | 10 |

10. Between the Sheets

| 1 | 2 | 3 | 4 | 5 | 6 | 7 | 8 | 9 | 10 |

11. Riding the Craze du Jour

| 1 | 2 | 3 | 4 | 5 | 6 | 7 | 8 | 9 | 10 |

12. Lying

| 1 | 2 | 3 | 4 | 5 | 6 | 7 | 8 | 9 | 10 |

13. Character Assassination

| 1 | 2 | 3 | 4 | 5 | 6 | 7 | 8 | 9 | 10 |

14. Stress Manipulation

| 1 | 2 | 3 | 4 | 5 | 6 | 7 | 8 | 9 | 10 |

15. Frontal Assault

| 1 | 2 | 3 | 4 | 5 | 6 | 7 | 8 | 9 | 10 |

Calculating Your Approximate Archetype

To see where you may fit, you need to calculate your ratings from the tactics tendencies you just rated. Each of the questions has a different multiplier for the number you circled. Make your calculations according to this formula:

	Your Rating	Multiply By	Total
Questions 1–3	_____	1	_____
Questions 4–8	_____	2	_____
Questions 9–11	_____	3	_____
Questions 12+	_____	4	_____
Grand Total:			_____

Next take your total score from the Self-Analysis in Chapter 3 and add it to your total here. This is your approximate persona rating, which simply shows your tendencies in terms of person-alities. Compare this to the ratings below to get an idea where of you stand.

Persona Tendency	Rating
Mindless Slugs	65–90
Hoppers	91–130
Survivalists	131–150
Apoliticals	151–200
Career Politician	201–350
Aggressors	351–475
Bosses	476+

Disclaimer

This is far from scientifically accurate. Age, political back-ground, and your own personally figure in strongly to this ele-ment. Age alone may help guide you toward either end of the spectrum, depending on experience and background as well as your own morals. This is aimed at giving you a very rough guideline as to where you may or may not fit. But in the end, your own review of the archetypes or personas may be the best way to determine what kind of individual you are—or want to be.

8

> In politics stupidity is not a handicap.
>
> **Napoléon**

ENDGAME

You've made it this far, and as a reward for climbing the mountain, some final pearls of wisdom are yours for the taking. This chapter has two major parts—one covering ways to defeat politics in your organization, and the other on the laws of cubicle warfare.

For those of you who want to survive the political firefights raging in your office, the section on how to beat politics is critical. If you are a manager, the reading is mandatory. This is the way that you can take cubicle warfare head-on and beat it, if you've got the guts.

And now for those of you corrupted by the Dark Side of the Force. If you bought and read this book so that you can be a better political player, make sure you read the first section, but just skim it so you can get to the fun part—the laws of warfare—simple guidelines to assist you with summarizing what has occurred thus far in the book.

HOW TO BEAT POLITICS

I once sat in a meeting at one of the Fortune 50 companies when we got a new manager. You don't survive long in a megacorporation without racking up a political body count, and this guy (according to my intelligence sources) was no exception.

He got up in front of all of us and said, "I've heard there's a lot of politics and backstabbing going on in this department. Now that I'm in charge, we aren't going to have any more of that kind of behavior."

Who died and made this geek God? Suppressing the urge to double over laughing took all my strength, but somehow I pulled it off. Within six months we had actually become *more* cutthroat in our activities as a department, and he was one of the major instigators. But every chance he got, he whined and bitched about the politics going on and how he had ordered it stopped.

There's no manager on this planet who can get up and command that office politics and cubicle warfare stop. There are some things that a manager of an organization can do to minimize political activity, to squelch it, but they never purge it completely.

This section is golden material for a manager who does not want to lead his or her people down the path of corruption but instead wants them in the office to do that work thing.

Don't Reward Politics

If you want to make sure that taking part in petty cubicle wars is not encouraged, don't reward those who do it. Rewards come in a lot of forms—praise, promotion, bonuses, and so on. If members of your staff are doing well but using every bit of political leverage to make things happen, you are not doing them or the rest of your staff any favors by endorsing and supporting those actions.

In fact, if you reward those who take part in political activity, you are sending a clear message to the rest of the staff. "If you want to get ahead, do whatever it takes and I'll treat you right for it."

Performance Is What Counts

So if you can't reward people for political ingenuity, what can you reward them for? How about doing their jobs and doing them well? Set realistic and obtainable goals for your people. Monitor their progress. Give them feedback and encouragement.

If you reward your people for their performance rather than their politics, you send a clear signal as to the behavior you want.

Punish Political Players

Do not crush, mutilate, bend, fold, or staple—but punish. This is the opposite of a reward and does not have to be a vicious attack or demotion of the employee in question. It does have to be direct and succinct, and it has to make very clear that the behavior in question (waging a cube war) is not the kind of action or activity that you endorse or support.

This is not an act of ruining someone's career. When your employees do something that you do not support, you owe it to them as their manager to tell them so that they can correct it. This may be nothing more than a verbal warning or, depending on the nature of the offense, it may be something more formal.

Almost every company has some rules and guidelines on progressive discipline, so check with the appropriate folks in HR for how to handle it. Remember one thing: The goal of this is to correct the inappropriate behavior (the political activity), not to get the employee terminated.

Manage Meetings and Cut Back Committees

It has never ceased to amaze me that many companies or firms don't train their managers how to correctly facilitate and run meetings. This is a large part of their job, but for the most part managers simply don't know how to do it or they don't do it correctly.

In this guide to beating politics, you need to do two things. First, learn how to run a meeting correctly and to facilitate it so that you get the most productivity out of the gathering. Second, take an active role in making sure that meetings or committees are not simply formed to allow managers to avoid making the tough decisions.

For the first, you need to get some facilitation training and practice. Go on, it's worth it. It is the best investment that you can get when it comes to your career and to controlling committees (Read: "breeding grounds of political fungus").

For the second element, use some common sense and avoid the temptation to throw together task forces and committees just so you don't have to do your job. It's not totally easy, but it is doable.

Provide Enough Work

Idle hands are the devil's workshop. Career office politicians and cubicle warriors often play the game because they have the time to do so. Your job as a manager is to make sure that your staff has plenty of business or work to do so that you minimize the time they have for office politics.

This does not mean burying them with work. It does mean making sure that they have enough work with short enough deadlines so that they are forced to focus on their work, as opposed to sabotaging careers, stealing faxes, and so on.

Focus Competition

Office politics comes from the urge to compete and win, to get ahead at any or all costs. This alone is not bad. However, in many offices the ability to move up is limited, which forces people to take extreme measures to make sure that they get those few open positions. In other words, stab everyone else in the back and crawl over their bodies to get that directorship or partnership or VP title.

Competition is normal and healthy. It just needs to be concentrated on business matters. If a position becomes available, don't be secretive about how you will select someone for it. Let the staff know that they will be rewarded for their work performance (sound familiar yet?) and that this is simply one of those

ut Everyone Else. . . . Managers often don't try to suppress office politics because "everyone else is doing it." This lemming's approach to management is based on the rationale that if everyone else in the company or firm is waging cubicle warfare with each other, it is impossible to stop without becoming a department of victims.
   Horse crap.

rewards. Do this, and your competing staff will concentrate on doing their best jobs in the office, rather than seeing who can post pictures of whom dirty dancing at the Christmas party.

Assign Authority with Responsibility

Matrix management and decades of weak-kneed managers in the workplace have led to people being able to have authority but no responsibility for their actions. This has to come to an end if you hope to weaken the political pull in your organization.

When people ask for authority to do something, you need to impress upon them they are *responsible* for it as well. If it goes wrong, they will be held accountable. If it goes well, they will be rewarded.

The concepts of responsibility and accountability are critical for managers to master. They are important. Without them, people feel free to act (or take part in politics) without fear of repercussions. Once they are held accountable, most managers take the power (authority) more seriously and aren't as willing to engage in petty cubicle warfare.

Managers who refuse to stop politics because no one else will are part of the problem. This is what saps the strength of the organizations from within, costing companies millions in lost productivity. Almost always, these managers have never tried to stop their political bloodletting because they lack the guts that God gave a sand flea and are unwilling (Read: "afraid") to take the risk.

Avoid Cubicle Warfare Yourself

Managers who say one thing and do another often seem more the norm than the exception. When trying to avoid cubicle warfare, however, you must lead from the front—lead by example. Don't ask your people to do something you are not willing to do yourself.

This does not mean that you have to become a monk, devoid of political interest. It does mean that you must minimize your office politics. Don't attempt high-profile political action that your subordinates will see. And above all, don't drag your staff into your political actions, even those employees whom you might be grooming for advancement. As you already know, the grapevine always prevails; your people will learn what you are doing and get a mixed message regarding political activity.

LAWS OF CUBICLE WARFARE: THE ART OF CUBE WAR

More than two thousand years ago the Chinese warrior philosopher Sun Tzu compiled a book of strategic principles. His *Art of War* has been translated thousands of times and is widely read as a guide for waging warfare. It is still required reading at military academies and by students of history—the principles hold up over time.

The list in this section of *Cubicle Warfare* will not, most likely, survive the ages like Sun Tzu's masterful work. (*Author's note: I'd like it to live on for 2,000 years given what the residual royalties would be, but that doesn't seem too hopeful.*) What this list does do is provide modern-era readers with a set of guidelines that may assist them as they attempt to eke out a survival in the dark halls of corporate monotony.

The list includes sets of rules for Attack, Defense, Dealing with Enemies or Foes, and Intelligence. Together these four areas represent the full suite of cubicle warfare rules. Combined with what you have read thus far in the text, these rules can help you to become a master strategist like Sun Tzu himself.

Rules of Attack

Attack when your opposition is weakest or least expects it. Remember, they will do the same to you.

Launching a political tactic in an area where you are undergunned and cannot hope to win is a waste of time and energy. There is no honor lost in a quick kill. Better to strike when enemies are down and finish the job rather than let them stab you in the back later on.

In defeat, attack. In victory, attack.

See the trend here?

The more others fight your battles for you, the better.

The more people who stand between you and your opponent, the less chance he or she has to see what you are really up to.

Always factor management's incompetence into your assaults.

Often overlooked in laying out cubicle warfare plans is the fact that some managers, when it comes to managing or leading, are idiots. Press that advantage where you can.

The Rule of Momentum: In any office, panic breeds panic.

If you win, start your next advance. People who are defeated are easy to convince to fail again.

Never engage in a political fight unless you stand to advance yourself from victory. Fighting to maintain the status quo is a waste of time and effort.

Do not attack if there is nothing for you to gain. You may end up drawing attention to yourself when it is least wanted or anticipated.

Never do the expected.

Most of your opponents live in the here and now. The more unconventional your attack, the more unique (beyond the pages of this book), the better your chance for success.

Everyone has a weak spot.

No one is a saint in the corporate world. Find that chink in the armor and run with it.

Fear in others means you're doing something right.

If you notice people trying to stay away from you or attempting to curry your favor, chances are you are doing well in your political wars.

It is always you against the rules. The key is to be in a position to make the rules in the first place.

No one in the known universe endorses office politics and backstabbing. By its very nature, office politics is something that is wrong. Be in a place to change the rules in case you get caught at some point.

You are only as good as your last victory or failure in the eyes of others.

The life span of memory in many companies is four to six months. If you wish to exploit a victory, you must do it quickly or it will be forgotten or corrupted by your enemies.

Technology is a double-edged sword.

For every advance that technology provides you in cubicle warfare, it also provides a weakness that your opponents will seek to exploit.

The more base or sinister the motive, the more cutthroat the tactic required.

If you want to be king, you must be willing to kill others in the court to get ahead. That is part of the price that power holds.

Lose a battle only when it positions you to achieve victory in the entire war.

Wars can be won even if battles are lost. Only concede defeat when it is to your long-term advantage.

If you're riding coattails to the top, make sure you're standing on more than one coat.

This is roughly akin to "Don't put all your eggs in one basket." Many a career has been hamstrung by people who didn't have the common sense to diversify their butt-kissing efforts.

Do not stop to mourn the dead.

The deep meaning in this is not to get caught up in the negative feelings that this kind of warfare generates. Don't stop and weep for those who have fallen. Either avenge them, laugh over their graves (empty desks), or become a victim yourself. Sitting around moping weakens your attacks.

Rules of Defense

The smaller your profile, the less of a target you are. Likewise, the larger the target, the easier it is to hit.

Enough said.

The more you try to hide a weakness, the more it stands out.

People are always watching you. If you try to hide something, someone will find out and investigate it even further. This is the nature of curiosity.

When all else fails, remember the scapegoat. Corollary: Always have a scapegoat or two in the wings.

My fault? No, it was Bob; Bob and Mary. Yeah, they're the ones who need to be taken down on this one.

Make no plans that cannot be changed.

Flexibility and the ability to adapt to a rapidly changing environment are crucial for employees and managers who hope to survive in corporations or firms today. If you cast your plans in concrete, you will almost certainly sink with them attached to your feet.

Use confusion and chaos—confuse your opposition.

While panic breeds panic on the attack, confusion breeds chaos on the defense. Sow the seeds of confusion with your enemies via the grapevine and you will weaken their support.

Self-preservation always prevails.

This will occur to you when all else fails. It is natural and instinctive. Keep in mind, this instinct will always force the need for some sort of a plan to preserve yourself. Shooting yourself in an underground bunker is not a viable option.

When all else fails, a lie implicating another will often work.

Sometimes a good scapegoat is hard to find. When one can't be found, fake one.

"No" is always an option. Buck's Corollary: Sometimes the best course of action is to do nothing.

People have gotten away from the basics. Don't get so reactive that you feel you must react to everything your enemies do. Sometimes the best thing you can do is sit back and see where things go all on their own—sometimes they go nowhere at all!

Never underestimate something that is simple and logical.

In other words, don't overlook the obvious. Many of those you fight in cubicle warfare are not sophisticated, and their tactics will reflect that. Just don't overlook something that is right in front of you.

Company-sponsored social gatherings are far from social.

The company or firm Christmas party is a hotbed of political activity—as is the summer picnic. For some reason, people tend to forget that fact when they've brought their spouses with them. Rather than be caught in incriminating photos table dancing in the nude on the CEO's desk, apply some gray matter to these occasions, all right?

Never underestimate the threat of legal action.

It's a world of lawyers and lawsuits. Companies hate them. Even a hint at such action can have great results.

Sleeping with someone on your staff is prostitution: there's always a price associated with the act.

No offense, but only a few people really sleep around in the office for the fun of it all. If you bed down one of your subordinates, you'd better be prepared to deal with the consequences of that tawdry thrill.

Budgets are rough guidelines and never come up until someone applies politics.

In the history of cubicle warfare, budget discrepancies have never surfaced unless an enemy has suggested something is amiss.

You can only burn your bridges to cut off pursuit once.

Well, maybe twice. If you have to hang someone out to dry, your victim is going to carry a grudge and want a little revenge. You can only do that twice or more if the person involved is *really* gullible.

For every good reorg, there were four that were total disasters.

Reorganization efforts cause rises in politics. Given this, you should accept the fact that only 25 percent of them actually accomplish anything productive.

Never become irreplaceable in your position.

Irreplaceable people are either totally expendable or totally unpromotable. Amateurs in cubicle warfare tend to want to be secure in the thought that they cannot be replaced. Usually they can and are or, worse yet, they are locked into a position for the rest of their lives.

Rules of Intelligence

There is more than one version of the truth. Rubie's Corollary: The truth is the truth. The perception of the truth is the spin. The spin can be controlled.

Truth is relative. Given enough supporting data (real or imaginary), truth can be manufactured.

A rumor can always defeat a ream of contradictory memos.

People like and believe a good rumor long before they trust anything that a corporate officer has written.

The one who controls communications controls the organization.

Duh.

You will never see the bullet that will kill you. You will, however, always see the gunman—who may be on your staff.

Don't get paranoid is the basis of this rule. You have no idea of what is running through the brains of those you are going up against. Just keep them in sight and that's half the battle.

Keep all plans secret. Confide your goals to people and they will be in charge.

One man's secret is a noose in another man's hands.

The greater the risk, the more you have to lose.

Want to be CEO in five months' time? Well you had better be willing to bet the farm. Those who would take you out would do so with such a vengeance that you'll be lucky if you survive to fight another battle.

The bigger the policy manual, the more political the office.

Rules breed politics like moisture breeds mold. The more rules and policies a company has, the more politics it has going that require the rules in the first place.

All employee agreements are evil.

These are documents drafted so that you, your thoughts, your body and soul are property of a company for a lifetime in exchange for the money that you have worked for. They are used in politics and only to remove employees—never to promote them.

Once a team meets its goals it will begin to self-destruct.

They key to this is to always make sure that new goals and objectives are in place. The less pressure a team or department has, the more time people have to wage cubicle warfare.

The less often a manager is in the office, the less loyal the staff is likely to be.

The era of a mobile workforce means that there is less supervision. If you want to defend your turf, you need to visit more than once a week.

The only good witness is the one you have dirt on.

Witnesses to your political skullduggery are a bad idea in the first place. If you have any, make sure you have them in your back pocket.

If you don't think about tomorrow, you won't survive today.

People don't think of the big picture daily. If you want to survive, you need to start.

Remember: No matter how ignorant you believe your management to be, somehow they got into their current position above you and most likely used politics to get there.

Management often displays a high degree of incompetence, but no matter what, those folks got there somehow. Either they have dirt, an ace up their sleeve, or slept their way to the top.

In the contemporary office, always assume that someone else is reading your e-mail.

This actually applies to everything you do in writing. Don't put anything in writing unless you are comfortable with others reading it—or trying to use it against you.

The more complex the security, the more holes there are in the fence.

Even in the most highly secured facilities, with lasers, card-accessed doors, and camera-monitored halls and rooms, a person working for minimum wage still empties the wastebaskets. In other words, there is always a way.

On Enemies and Foes

Those who crave power the most are the most dangerous foes.

Power is a hunger that consumes many. The greater the hunger, the more deadly the person consumed by it.

Allies are better than enemies but should be treated with the same care.

In laymen's terms, don't trust even those who claim to be your good friends. We're all friendly until jobs, positions, and power come into play. Remember, Caesar was killed by a dozen good friends.

Use others or they will use you.

No person can stand totally alone. Either involve others or they will suck you into their political ploys.

The only totally vanquished enemy is one who is dead or left for another career. Blaine's Subsidiary Rule: Dead is dead. Everything else can and may come back to haunt you.

Never turn your back on someone you've defeated unless they leave the company or are in a coffin. People come back from defeat, and revenge is a good motivation tool.

Keep your number of enemies low and always keep them in sight.

Don't try to take on the entire world. Concentrate your efforts on the 20 percent of the political players who can or will affect your life.

Cornered rats are hard to kill; always leave an enemy a way out . . . but never an easy way.

If you trap people and don't leave them some way to exit and save even a little face, they will come at you as if they have nothing to lose. Why? Because they don't have anything to lose. Always give your enemy a chance to leave the field of battle unless you are assured they are willing to leave the company or firm.

Your company's external competition is enemy number two—number one is a peer or subordinate.

Never just look at your peers as potential enemies. Those who are below you are a threat as well.

No one is 100 percent honest with every report—especially if money is involved.

If you are looking for a way to take on an enemy, look to the reports he or she is responsible for creating.

The more priorities change, the more chances there are for politics.

Change is constant in companies today. The more change you attempt to implement as a manager, the more opportunity you provide potential enemies to wage politics.

Be wary of people who are so stupid they risk their career for no gain.

One word: Sociopaths.

Never trust any subordinate who's willing to take a bullet meant for you.

People who seem so blindly loyal that they will risk their career so that you can live are people who cannot ever be fully trusted.

No one seeks your counsel unless they seek to advance themselves.

Forget friendship. When peers come to you to ask your advice, they most likely are trying to drag you into a political dogfight.

Always assume your political opponent has less scruples or morals than you.

Expect the worst. Exploit everything else when you can.

No one is as stupid as they seem. Pardoe's Clause: In some cases that's just not possible.

A master politician will appear as bright as Forrest Gump to the masses, but in reality may be deadly killer. Never be fooled by ignorance. Death wears many masks.

Age relates to success in politics—NOT!

Just because people have been in your company or firm forever does not mean they are master politicos. In reality, they may be mindless slugs who have simply been lucky thus far or who have barely cheated death throughout their careers.

Beware anything obvious.

If it's obvious, it is most likely dangerous. Ninety percent of cubicle warfare involves tactics or variants that have been done thousands of times before. Watch and be wary of these things.

Given enough time, some foes will defeat themselves.

Ever play air hockey? Much of the time the goals against you are caused by your own hand accidentally knocking the puck in. The same applies in cubicle warfare. Sometimes the best thing to do is sit back and let others and the powers at be do the damage for you. But remember, don't pass up a chance to jump in for the kill!

MASTERY

I have lived long enough to satisfy both nature and glory.

Julius Caesar

At this point you're ready to graduate from the equivalent of Officer's Candidate School and lead your troops into battle in the never-ending cubicle war. No longer are you the raw recruit who started reading this book, but instead you are now at least somewhat seasoned. You've studied the strategies and tactics that make up this war. You've looked at yourself and the battlefield—you've stared into the eyes of your enemies and shown them that you have no fear in your heart.

You are now qualified, having digested this book, to lead others into battle. Yes, there are nuances and twists that your foes will create that are not covered in this book, but you now have enough weapons at your disposal to stand victorious at the end of the fight. In cubicle warfare, the last one standing is the victor.

If you started this journey as a person who wanted to become a warlord, a cubicle warrior extreme, congratulations. You now see how office politics play out. You should now have a good interpretation, if you didn't already, as to how low individuals will go to advance themselves. You can jump into a fight and at least stand a chance of surviving if not being victorious. You are now armed and equipped for the struggle that will consume your entire career and life.

If you have been reading this book to learn the ways of war to prevent war, you have had a stirring glimpse into what drives today's companies. It's been blunt and brutal, but if nothing else you are armed with the information necessary to do the most important thing you can in an office consumed by politics—survive.

And in the end, survival is what this book is all about. There have been millions of victims of tactics from backstabbing to brownnosing. No one will ever know the depth of depravity that some have used to ruin or soil their peers' careers. Office politics is the kind of stuff that makes the Dark Side of the Force seem like a mild headache. But if you can take this information and survive this weird yet oddly interesting behavior, then you've accomplished something really important. You are not a mindless slug but an individual—a person who refuses to be more than a brainless cog in the political machine that runs most corporations.

And, in that dignity, you have achieved more success than any mere title can provide.

INDEX

A Journey into the Heroic Environment

A Personal Guide to Creating
a Work Environment Built on Shared Values

Rob Lebow

U.S. $13.00
Can. $17.95
ISBN: 0-7615-0904-6
paperback / 224 pages

"I loved this simple, powerful book. Buy it!" —Harvey Mackay, author of *Swim with the Sharks Without Being Eaten Alive*

Two strangers' chance encounter leads us all on a compelling journey into the fascinating and stimulating new Shared Values work environment, where all workers and their ideas are treated with dignity and respect. This modern business classic has been newly revised and updated to reflect 25 years of research—including 17 million surveys from 40 countries—into what people really want in their workplace. A quiz allows you to evaluate your work environment's capacity for Shared Values.

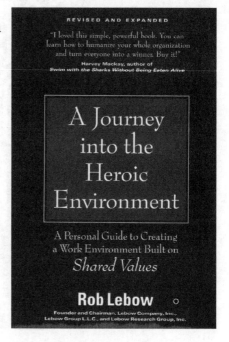

Visit us online at http://www.primapublishing.com

Strategic Job-Jumping

How to Get from Where You Are to Where You Want to Be

Julia Hartman

U.S. $13.00
Can. $17.95
ISBN: 0-7615-1023-6
paperback / 176 pages

In today's volatile job market, change is inevitable. Success isn't. You need to plan—*now*—how you will take charge of your career path for greater financial security and job satisfaction. *Strategic Job Jumping* gives you the tools you need to:

- Package your skills for higher-level jobs
- Present your job-jumping experience as an asset
- Skip rungs as you climb your career ladder
- Network on and off the job—and online
- Negotiate compensation packages and entry and departure bonuses
- Maintain insurance coverage
- And more!

Strategic Job Jumping puts you in control of your future!

Visit us online at www.primapublishing.com